# MANDATORY GREATNESS

## THE 12 LAWS OF DRIVING
## EXCEPTIONAL PERFORMANCE

Dale Dauten

&

"J.T." O'Donnell

Published by
LUMINA MEDIA

Mandatory Greatness.

Cover and Interior Design: Chris Molé Design

For information, contact Dale Dauten at dale@dauten.com or J.T. O'Donnell at jt@careerhmo.com.

*For Jeri Dauten, who first taught me standards, and still does.*

DALE DAUTEN

*To my father John and mother Kay. Thanks for being my "mandatory greatness" parents first, my friends second.*

*To my daughters Cassidy and Skylar. I hope this book inspires you both when you are managers someday.*

*To my husband Eric. Thank you for loving me the way you do.*

J.T. O'DONNELL

*In everyone's life, at some time, our inner fire goes out.*

*It is then burst into flame by an encounter with another human being.*

*We should all be thankful for those people who rekindle the inner spirit.*

~ Albert Schweitzer

*Our chief want in life is somebody who shall make us do what we can.*

~ Emerson

# THE 12 LAWS

1.  You and your team are a commodity product until you prove otherwise.

2.  Leadership is a magnificent intolerance.

3.  Bureaucracies evolve; organizations devolve.

4.  Criticism is a compliment.

5.  Never trust a manager who loves everything you do.

6.  Stop and smell the roses, yes, but sometimes you've got to stop and smell the fish.

7.  They ALWAYS KNOW.

8.  Understand who's ready for a not-ready assignment.

9.  Fear is your friend (and "Are you crazy?" is that friend winking at you).

10. Choose "respected" over "liked." The love comes later.

11. If you're certain, you've wimped out.

12. One sentence is worth a thousand meetings.

# PREFACE

It started with me winning a prize—and being disappointed about it. What happened is that I entered a charity raffle and when they called to tell me I'd won, I got fired up because I thought they meant the big prize, the trip to Paris. No. They meant second prize, which was a "career coaching session" with some woman I'd never heard of. I pretended to be pleased, of course, but I was rolling my eyes. At the time, if I'd been given the choice, I would have opted for something, anything else…say, steak knives, like in that *Glengarry Glen Ross* movie. I said so, and it became a joke around the office; someone even giftwrapped a cheap set of steak knives and left it on my desk.

The week after hearing I'd won the raffle, I got a call from that coach I'd never heard of, Yvonne Wolfe. I was skeptical, assuming that the coaching was really a "free trial," after which she'd try to sell me on signing up for her services. So as I answered her many, many questions about my work, I assumed she was doing the old "ask, don't sell" sell. I played along.

Eventually, she said that she wanted to come in to observe me at the office. This sounded like a pretty big time commitment for both of us, and because I was still imagining that she'd try to sign me up for regular coaching, I decided to give her an out: "I should warn you that my company has a freeze on all outside consulting, including coaching." As I said this, I was half hoping that she'd back off and we'd end up forgetting the whole idea. Instead, she chuckled.

"First," she informed me, "no company is going to pay what I get paid except to coach those at the highest level, and second, I'm booked up, I have a waiting list, and I'm not taking new names. So I suggest we both focus and make the day a useful one because this is a one-shot deal. Deal?"

I chuckled right back, then agreed, still thinking like a sales guy and telling myself, "She's really working the 'scarcity' gambit. Impressive."

# CHAPTER ONE:
## My Inadvertent Mediocrity

### My Brilliant Morning

Yvonne showed up early and settled into a corner of my office, telling me to pretend she wasn't there. She was classy, older—she might have been, say, Diane Sawyer's sister. She was friendly, but not pals-y. I had the feeling that she was not easily impressed, which was a worry because I'd learned in the interim that she knew my boss's boss.

Because of that connection, I made sure to look like a guy who should be promoted. I even brought in one of those little caffeine-laced energy drinks, wanting to be sure to be extra upbeat. And I was. Positive. Helpful. Supportive. Funny. An active listener and dispenser of knowledge. It was a great show, and I found myself thinking that if only I could keep up that level of brilliance, it wouldn't be long till I was running the place.

She, however, said nothing along the way, did not react, just took notes. I confess I found it a bit off-putting-- when you score a touchdown, you want to hear some applause.

The morning passed, and then it was my turn to listen and take notes. She closed the door and pulled her chair to the side of my desk.

## The Gift You Don't Want But Need

She bit her upper lip with her lower teeth and stared at me before saying, "I'm going to give you a gift today."

When I smiled, she gave back a tight, unhappy half-smile, then added, "It's something you *don't* want but I believe you need."

Still feeling high from my performance, I joked, "It's not socks, is it?"

Ignoring that one, she said, "It's something rare. The gift is complete honesty."

That's when I figured it out...or thought I had. I thought she was being mock-serious, so she could then say something like, "You are a-maz-ing!" and break into grins and high-fives. Naturally, I urged her to press on.

"If you continue doing what I saw today, this is my prediction for your future: You're going to be passed over for the big promotions. Instead, you'll make some small advances in status and pay-- which is good until it's bad, which is when the next big recession hits and well-paid middle managers get axed and you'll be out of work at the worst time."

I mean, *WHAT*? I kept my composure and replied calmly, trying to make light of the slight, "So when do I get the gift?"

"You're getting it. The easiest thing for me to do would be to tell you how great you're doing and then maybe offer up a few 'tips' or 'pointers.' That way, you'd like me and think I was a good coach, and I'd be out of here in ten minutes. Instead, I'm going to give you the gift of deep criticism, of telling you that you're not doing anything special and thus you are destined to lead an average team and have an average career."

Without even giving me time to absorb that punch, she pressed on, "You'll resent the suggestions and argue with me, but I'm going to take the chance because you might be one of the few who is ready."

I was a bit annoyed with this and said, "Is this some coaching trick—insult the people you work with?"

"Oh. Did I insult you? I didn't mean to." Here I don't think she was being entirely honest. "My prediction," she continued, "was simply that you're going to have an average career—and, okay, I suppose, in our culture, 'average' is an insult. The culture is full of relentless positive reinforcement and the promulgation of high self-esteem."

Feeling testy, I replied aridly, "So what's the option—negative reinforcement and low self-esteem?"

She smiled, a genuine one, liking the challenge. "Here's one thing I can tell you that you'll like hearing: You could be special. You have it in you." She was right—that sounded much better, although I was still reeling from her first comments, so I was expecting her to add, "Just like everyone else."

Instead she continued, "However, you don't become special by doing ordinary things and having everyone tell you how terrific you are. All parents applaud when the toddler uses the potty, calling in the other parent to look at the little poop. But if you're still applauding when the kid is 25, something is wrong. And not with the kid."

I was going to ask how that might apply to me, but realized that I didn't need to. All I had to do was think back through the work I'd done earlier in the day, the work she'd watched, which included a performance review where I ladled out the congratulations like Mr. Smiley Positivo. Why? Because the guy had done his job...mostly. He'd done most of what he was paid to do, without zest or innovation, and I'd treated him like...well, I had applauded the potty. Slap.

## The Choice

She read the frustration in my face and said, "Let's get away from taking it personally. Let's make it a business issue instead. Let's say you own a small business and you are working hard and making a decent income. Then one day, you win a session with a business consultant, and they let you pick one of these...

- An uplifting session, where she will come in and reinforce everything you're doing right, then give you some pointers and tell you some inspiring stories about sticking with it and overcoming obstacles. That's one choice.

or

- She will come in and say, 'You're screwing up, doing a lot wrong. Change your approach and you could be making twice as much and not working as many hours."

She rolled her hand toward me, "Your pick."

I smiled and raised my hands in surrender.

"The hard truth is that most people are told they are great while being shown how to be ordinary. I'm going to tell you you're ordinary and show you how to be great. "

I objected: "Hey, you left out the third way-- how about a consultant who tells me I'm great and then shows me how to make twice as much?"

This prompted her to point at me and say, "You know what? That's how I started out my career, trying for that approach. Then she summarized her career revelation...

———————

"I spent twenty years in corporate life, working long hours and getting the little breaks, but not the big ones. Like most women of my generation, I blamed it on being a woman. But then I saw some women who were advancing much more rapidly than I was. Hmmm. Maybe it wasn't being a woman, but being a mom. And by that I mean that I was the supportive, understanding mother of the departments I ran. Meanwhile, I went to goal-setting seminars and got an MBA and studied successful leaders, and still my department never did anything special. And *that* was why I wasn't getting the big breaks—the *not being special*. It wasn't anything I was, but what I wasn't. I was an ambitious manager with the same old tools and thinking as everyone else. I was inadvertently mediocre, just like you."

———————

Sighing, she seemed to be disgusted by the manager she used to be, and I wasn't thrilled myself, being inducted into Club Mediocre. She added, "I used to tell people, in essence, 'You're fabulous, and I love your work—BUT I believe you could do even more.' You know what people hear when you say that? They think: 'I'm doing great. She loves me. I passed the test, so why should I work harder?' Picture going to the DMV and the clerk says, 'You passed, but you seem like you could do much more—if you go back home and study for a couple more weeks I think you could get 100%.' Would you come back in two weeks or just take your new license?"

## Team Leader or Team Mom

By now she was getting into it, the words coming fast. "And here's the truth: In most departments, performance devolves...*de*volves. The person who does the least work becomes the definition of what's acceptable. Performance devolves to that level because most people only work as hard as they have to. Sounds obvious, but if you keep it in mind, I think it will change forever the way you manage."

"That sounds so negative," I objected, even though I suspected she was right. "So you're going to tell me to manage by fear— 'Do this or you're fired?'"

She chuckled. "Your output would go up—yes, yes, it would- – but that's not what I'm going to suggest. When I said that people work as hard as they have to, it's *not only* as hard as they have to in order to keep their jobs. It's also to make their bonuses, or get to work on a pet project, or get promoted, or not let down the team. We'll get to finding the right motivators, but for now I want you to understand there's a danger of going from being the team leader to being the team mom.

And, I should make clear, this happens to as many men as women. If you're the department's team mom, you're sweet and understanding and wonderfully likable, and everyone brings their problems to you, and your job becomes making sure that nothing goes wrong. And that's how you get the little breaks. *The big breaks go to those who make things go right; the little breaks go to those who make sure things don't go wrong.*

"And, remember this, *your team wants you to be the team mom.* That's the default setting. *That's what happens to you if you don't take a stand and insist on being the leader.*"

## The Three Types— The Smart-Ass, Kiss-Ass and Hard-Ass

I was impressed with her conviction and her logic, but I can't say that I was ready to change my life. Maybe I was a bit too easy on myself and my team, but we were doing okay and I liked being likable. I just didn't see myself as merely a team mom. So at that point in our conversation, I was like the customer who is very impressed by the sales presentation, but still wasn't going to buy.

I had only half-realized my inner objections when some intuition made Yvonne stop and challenge me. "You're just playing along now. That's not good enough for me. Let's see if this makes a difference. Let's say for argument that there are only three types of managers in the world: There's the smart-ass, the kiss-ass and the hard-ass.

"Within each type, there's a continuum from low to high— from obnoxious to charming, from unlovable to lovable—but only those three basic types. And I'm going to name some people, and you tell me which of the types they are."

I wanted to debate her categories, but she insisted I play along. And when I asked for more detail, she'd only say that what defines the three is the fundamental focus:

- **The smart-ass** is focused on himself, on bringing the joke or zinger, on having all the answers.
- **The kiss-ass is** focused on getting along, on being positive and likable, on giving people what they want and telling them what they want to hear.
- **The hard-ass is** obsessed with standards, numbers, and deadlines.

With that as background, she asked me, "Picturing those three types, which one was Steve Jobs?"

I knew his reputation for being demanding and difficult, so it was an easy choice: "Hard."

"How about Sam Walton?"

He came across as "country," but I knew that he had been a vicious competitor who grabbed off every good idea he came across and who hammered home the numbers. "Hard."

"How about Henry?" She meant the executive at my company who was the rising star, my boss's boss. This guy was a charmer and was well-liked, but he had driven his group to terrific numbers by having a reputation for driving down prices and cutting deadlines and by pushing employees, who all joked about how difficult he was—but they joked with deep affection. I nodded to indicate that he was, like the others, in the "hard" group.

It took a while to find some other leaders that I knew enough about to rate, and I don't remember them all, but there were the obvious ones, like Jack Welch and Martha Stewart, and the more surprising ones, like Oprah Winfrey—all placed in the hard-ass category.

"Now, she said, what about *you*?"

There was no way I could count myself as hard. I was always understanding and let things slide. And while I like to joke around, no one has ever called me a smart-ass. Which left the last group, the last one I wanted to be in, so I said, "There must be another group."

She laughed. "Well, there's dumb-ass. I left that one out because so few dumb-ass managers survive, and you certainly aren't one of them."

So, as I fought against it, there it was, this hard truth...

I was going around trying to be liked by everyone, letting things slide, finding a way to tell people what they wanted to hear —Mr. Positive, Mr. Compliment, Mr. Assume-The-Best, Mr. Close-Enough—in short, Mr. Softy. I was playing the role of the kiss-ass and didn't even know it, at least not till that moment. Slap.

And knowing what I had become pissed me off. I was ready to try something—everything—different. Whatever she was selling, I was buying.

## Resigning From Club Mediocre

"What I have observed," she explained, "is that virtually every successful leader is in the hard group. That doesn't mean that there aren't lots of successful people in the smart-ass category; it's just that they tend to be experts in their professions-- lawyers, doctors, engineers, professors. They sometimes get promoted into leadership roles, but the truth is, people don't want to follow a smart-ass. And there are lots of kiss-ass people in those same professions, and plenty in middle management. They tend to be nice people, and so I hate to see them end up where they end up: disqualified from the big breaks."

I brought the conversation back to Henry, the guy in our company who is the star, the guy everyone knows is going to end up running our company or a better one. "I just don't think of him as a Hard-Ass. He's so down-to-earth and polite, and he's involved in charity work and always gives other people credit. How is that 'hard'?"

"When I read the Stieg Larsson novels…" She asked a question with her eyes and I told her that although I hadn't read them, I knew the books she meant, *The Girl with the Dragon Tattoo* and the others. "…the heroine, Lisbeth, says at one point that she likes 'cocky devils' and detests 'pompous jerks,' pointing out that there's only a subtle difference. She doesn't attempt to define the difference; it's just something she feels. I found myself putting down the book to ponder that one and decided that it's a matter of focus. The pompous jerk loves himself, while the cocky devil loves a challenge. The one says, 'I'm terrific; admire me' while the other says, 'I'm terrific, and you are too. Let's do something exciting together.' You see where I'm going?"

I wasn't sure I did, but said yes.

"The hard/soft/smart distinction is about fundamental work focus. Beyond that is the human dimension, which includes style and personality. You can be a lovable smart-ass, or you can be a smart-ass who's an obnoxious know-it-all cynic."

She rummaged in her bag, one of those purse/briefcase thingies, and came up with a set of papers. "Here's something I'm writing where I described one classic leader. See if it fits Henry [my boss's boss]...

*He was charming... and demanding... a lovable tyrant. Like many of the best leaders, he was feared in the best way: the employees didn't fear HIM; they feared LETTING HIM DOWN, feared failing to live up to the reputation for exceptional work that he protected with a ferocity that would impress a tigress with a toothache.*"

"YES! That's so *him*," I agreed. "And because of it, all the best people want to work for him. It's like trying to get into Harvard or Stanford—you know that if you work for him, you've got a future."

"The CEO of Harrah's casinos, Gary Loveman, who's a former Harvard professor, told me that his best career advice is, 'Don't be the smartest person in the company.' What he meant is that you need to be around people who are going to lift you up, to pull you and push you."

I asked how I could get to work for a rising star manager, and she said, "You know that old bit about 'it takes one to know one'; there's something similar with high-achievers—it takes one to get hired by one."

Naturally I wanted to know how to get myself into that group.

She gave me a long, sad look, then said, "When was the last time one of the people you worked with said to you, *'Are you crazy?'*"

"Well... Never."

"That's where we start."

# CHAPTER TWO:

## The 12 Laws

But that isn't where we started. Yvonne told me that she wanted to review her notes and that I should answer email and phone calls for a half hour. She explained, "I know it's fallen out-of-favor, but I like to sit quietly and think before I offer opinions."

I offered her the use of a nearby conference room and I was relieved when she accepted. I confess to feeling like the mouse put in the cage with the big snake. When I joined her in the conference room, 30 minutes later to the minute, she said, "Here's the rest of my gift to you." She handed me a single sheet from a legal pad where she had written twelve items she titled "The 12 Laws."

(Even now, years later, I still have that sheet of paper. I put it in a plastic sleeve and keep it on my desk. It soon became a joke with my colleagues, and when I would say, "Number four," the employee would sigh, knowing what I was about to do and why. Or I'd say "Number six," and he would start to sweat. That actually proved point Number twelve, but it took me months to fully realize it.)

The next page shows what she wrote, a few dozen words but plenty...oh my, *plenty*...enough to change just about every-thing about how I worked, enough to propel me from "liked" to "respected."

# THE 12 LAWS

1. You and your team are a commodity product until you prove otherwise.

2. Leadership is a magnificent intolerance.

3. Bureaucracies evolve; organizations devolve.

4. Criticism is a compliment.

5. Never trust a manager who loves everything you do.

6. Stop and smell the roses, yes, but sometimes you've got to stop and smell the fish.

7. They ALWAYS KNOW.

8. Understand who's ready for a not-ready assignment.

9. Fear is your friend (and "Are you crazy?" is that friend winking at you).

10. Choose "respected" over "liked." The love comes later.

11. If you're certain, you've wimped out.

12. One sentence is worth a thousand meetings.

# CHAPTER THREE:
## Why "Hard" Is Required

She waited while I skimmed the list and she smiled at my confusion, promising that it would all be clear before the day was done.

"You come across as a very nice guy," she said, and I could tell she was *not* offering up a compliment. "I imagine that everyone thinks of you as a friend, maybe even as 'family.'" With that last word she let a tang of sarcasm leak in.

"Guilty," I said, still keeping it light.

"There are many places to find friendship, but few to find leadership. It's leadership that's in short supply-- a zillion 'leaders' but little leadership. Let's work on just what *leadership* means. Let's consider whether you're really leading your team." Here she asked me a couple of questions about my department and what we do. I explained that I headed training for our mid-sized national company. She then asked, "So how good is your team? How do you stack up to other training teams around the country?"

This was not something I spent time thinking about. I explained that we hadn't done benchmarking for our group, but added with justifiable pride, "I keep up. I attend national conferences and read the best blogs and publications. Given our size and budget limitations, we do great work. I can say..." and here I tapped the conference table for emphasis, "that we are living up to our commitment to be a world-class department."

I expected some encouragement, or at least some acknowledgment that I was a leader with a goal and a mission. Come on.

## The Two Causes of Mediocre Management

But no, she gave a look like the one Diane Sawyer gives after reporting that some politician was just accused of something shameful, a look that says, "Does no one ever learn anything?" Then she added this...

"Here are the two most common causes of mediocre management:

Cause number one is 'World Class,' and

Cause number two is 'Hire good people and get out of the way.'"

Before I could object, much less find a cross to hold in front of me (because this was management blasphemy if I'd ever heard it), she casually continued, "Let's start with world class. How do you work at being world class?"

I reiterated that I keep up on my reading and my professional associations, then boasted, "We take the best ideas from around the world and bring them right back here and put them to work."

She nodded. "Notice what you said there, that you 'keep up' on what's going on elsewhere. Keeping up is being a good follower. And that's the problem with 'world class' as a goal—it's a commitment to keeping up. So you're committed to being a follower."

"Not at all," I responded. "We're taking the best ideas and bringing them together. We aren't just imitating, we're creating a new synthesis." I liked how that sounded. How about you? Good point, right? Well, 'pop' went that pretty self-image bubble...

"That sounds so-o good," she replied, inviting me into her logic trap. "That's why everyone is doing it. Everyone is grabbing hold of the same new ideas, the same best practices. And if you're doing what everyone is doing, what does that make you?"

I thought it was a rhetorical question, but she was waiting for me to pull the trigger on my own ego suicide. "It makes me like everyone else."

"Said another way, it leads you to being *average* or maybe *high-level average*. Best practices and world class are the Sirens of mediocrity. Do you remember your *Ulysses*?"

Here I was pleased to not be a complete ignoramus, having done a major paper in school on just that subject. "Yes, as his ship approached the Sirens, Ulysses knew that upon hearing their call he and his sailors would leap into the sea, driven mad by their desire to join the Sirens. So he had his men put wax in their ears and then tie him to the mast so that he could hear them without breaking free."

At last she looked the tiniest bit impressed. "In your case," she said, "you need to hear the Sirens of best practices because you need to grab those ideas and adopt them. You have to keep up. But you can't stop there—you have to sail on. You can't believe that being world class is all there is. You have to be special. You have to do things that will land you on the cover of those publications you're reading. You have to be the one they want to speak. You do that by experimenting, not following. THAT's leadership."

## Improvement Isn't Leadership

She let that sink in and then added, "It isn't just you. In fact, the good news is that almost everyone is content to be the same sort of best practices follower that I'm describing. And that's a *huge* opening for you."

She continued by saying...

———————

"You start by understanding that improvement isn't leadership. Every decent manager and every decent training department is improving, and that's *good,* but often *not good enough.* When you hear about a business going out of business and meet people who worked there, they will invariably talk about how they were improving and just ran out of time and money. *We're improving… We're improving… We're obsolete.*"

———————

She added, "With internal departments like yours, you may not have the same marketplace death threat, but still, the same principle is there and now you know why I started the list of Laws with, *You are a commodity product until you prove otherwise.*

"And by *you*, I mean your career, your team, your department, your division, your company, and its products and services. The danger is thinking you're special when you're not. That's why the *burden of proof* is on *you* to prove you're not a commodity." She stopped herself and, looking concerned, asked, "Do we need to review why it is that you do NOT want to be a commodity product?"

"I'm clear on that one," I said. But she only raised an eyebrow a fraction of an inch, and I knew that she meant for me to prove it so I added, "If you're a commodity product then you're not seen as different or special. You're totally replaceable and at the lowest possible cost."

"Exactly. And here's the trick: *Everyone says he or she is different and most even believe it.*"

She went on to tell me about a consultant in Louisiana who'd impressed her—Mike Manes. She told of hearing him give a speech to insurance agents. The relevant part went something like this:

(Manes to insurance agents) "I go to your website, and it lists all the types of insurance you offer and it says that you have competitive rates. Then it says that what sets your agency apart is that you really care about your customers. Next, I pull out my computer and ask it to find nearby insurance agencies, and there are twenty of them within five miles. And I look at their websites, and guess what they say? What sets

25

them apart is that they really care about their customers. So I call you up and tell you that all the sites say the same thing about really caring. You say, 'Yeah, but we *really mean it.*' Then I call all the other agents, and guess what they all say? 'We *really mean it.*'"

She let that little ice pick of a story work its way into my consciousness, and I got it, that the danger isn't just the failure to differentiate; it is believing that you are different when you aren't, the opiate of the career masses. Later, I would understand that this is one reason you have to be hard, to pull off the blanket of self-satisfaction.

## The Anti-Commodity Logic

I jumped ahead and asked the Big Question: "So how do I get to be different?"

She answered me with me a story...

"My husband and I go to the lecture series put on by *National Geographic* where we heard a photographer named David Doubilet. At the end of his talk, someone asked him, 'How can I get a job like yours?' He responded by recalling his own start with the magazine. As a young man, he put together a portfolio of his best work and took it to one of the editors, who flipped through, closed the portfolio and sat silent for what Doubilet recalls as 'at least two minutes.' The editor then shrugged and said, 'There's nothing new here.'"

(She interrupted her story about this photographer to point out that these words must have stung. After all, he was just a kid, and the guy whacked his hopes. But then again, he should be forever grateful that he had given his portfolio to someone who was willing to give a tough assessment. Had he encountered the usual polite "positive reinforcement," he would have done more of the same, entered into Inadvertent Mediocrity and never escaped.)

Continuing, she quoted Doubilet as explaining that when aspiring photographers approach *National Geographic,* they get asked some version of the question, Why should you get an assignment? He said, "Typically the would-be employee responds with something like, 'I'll do anything, go anywhere. I'll risk my life. I'll be eaten by crocodiles or lions...anything.' That, he explained, is the wrong answer. What's the right answer? "I know one photographer who said, 'I'm getting really interested in cannibalistic butterflies. That was a right answer.'"

She smiled and said, "So there's your answer about how to be different. Cannibalistic butterflies."

Okay, I got it. Being different was up to me. *I was a commodity product until I proved otherwise.*

But where did that bit of knowledge get me? Instead of being content and self-satisfied, I was frustrated and annoyed with myself. Then again, she *was* a big-deal career coach, so I figured she could do more than talk about butterflies. So I asked for suggestions on finding my way out of commoditization. Instead of butterflies, I got socks. Which is ironic considering that my first joke when she said she was about to give me a gift was to mention socks. But, get this...after really understanding it, this story changed my life. Later, when I told Yvonne how much this one had meant to me, she introduced me to Jim Potts, and I got him to tell the story to me directly, with all the detail of a Southern storyteller, and it goes like this:

Along with his son Darrell and daughter-in-law Teena, Jim Potts owns a pair of stores in Arkansas called Lewis and Clark Outfitters. They sell hiking and camping gear in their retail stores and also have a line of products they sell through Sam's Club stores. Theirs is not a big, national success story—not yet—but a good one. Over the past two years their sales have quadrupled.

How'd they do it? When they opened the first store, the senior Potts didn't have much product expertise to offer customers: "I didn't understand the technical specs on the bikes or anything else in the store, so I decided to focus my attention on the one product I did understand: socks." He called the company that makes SmartWool socks and told them that he intended to become their number one store. They told him that he'd do well to sell a thousand pair a year. His quixotic response: "I can sell that many in a week."

His record is 1,320 pair in one weekend.

How did he do it? He made a challenge of getting every customer who came in the store to try on a pair. He called the folks at SmartWool and said, "What percent of people who try on your socks buy them?" They didn't know. So he told them it was 89 percent and asked for help with the cost of the un-purchased pairs (which the store gives to employees).

Eventually, Potts, sock expert, went directly to the factory and said, "Make me a better sock." They said, "Fine, but we need a million-dollar order." And that's when he persuaded the folks at Sam's Club to carry his new brand, OmniWool, and that became the first of several of Potts' products they carry.

Potts always had a big dream, but it started with one little item, a seemingly ordinary one that he decided was **not** going to be a commodity. He wasn't about to be one, either.

## Finding the "And"

About that story Yvonne concluded, "Not just every entrepreneur, but every employee in every company needs an *and*—'He's a great employee AND, oh boy, does he know socks.' We may belittle specialists for 'knowing more and more about less and less,' but when we need help, that's exactly the guy we turn to."

What I understood was that being competent was essential, but only that; it was merely a job requirement. I now understood that I didn't need to be different in everything, didn't need to change everything. All I needed was my "and," and then I needed to help everyone who worked for me find theirs.

## Follow The Energy

"How do you decide on the *and*?" I asked.

Here she turned Zen master and said, "As you understand the other principles, your distinction will appear."

*What?*

She saw the frustration and disappointment in my face and added, "To quote the great blues guitarist, Lightnin' Hopkins, 'Whatever you is, be that.'"

I waited for her to smile, but nope, nada. So, I decided, I've got to figure it out for myself, that if my specialty was going to be real it had to be "whatever I is." Sounds important, but where did it get me?

Then, seeing me struggling with the idea, she finally relented. "Okay. You have to find *the part of your work that gives you the most energy and follow it*. There is where you find your specialty. Most people think of being different and think of something visible, often some gimmick. So let me give you an example to put that idea in its place."

> "I gave a speech in Tampa and included some points on not being a commodity. After my speech, one of the attendees told me that his hobby was flying radio-controlled helicopters and how one company, ReadyHeli, had made itself distinctive simply by sending out mints with orders. Yes, mints.

> "Every time you get an order sent to you, you get a mint or two, with a wrapper that has the company name and logo. These aren't anything special, just high-end butter-mints. Big deal. But he insisted that people collect them. He told me, 'People post pictures online of how many mints they have. It's a status symbol.'

> "Curious, I went to the company's website and saw that the list starts with the old, boring stuff—excellent customer service and great product selection. Snooze. Important, of course, but everybody says it so there's no differentiation potential. Then there are these:

> - Sponsoring many fun fly events. [The web site has contests, including a "best crash video."]

> - The 'ReadyHeli Mints.'

- Feeding the [helicopter] addiction fast, by shipping our customers' orders out the same day."

Yvonne continued, "I called the founder of ReadyHeli, John Greco, who explained that he started the company out of his own hobbyist frustration at being unable to get repair parts quickly and easily. And the contests were a natural extension of a fellow hobbyist/addict creating an isn't-this-cool business for peers. So they really were different—they didn't just say they cared but proved it by same-day shipping and by creating a site that fellow hobbyists really wanted to visit.

"And then there are those mints. I asked John if he thought they really were important. He laughed and said, 'God forbid we forget to include a mint with the order. We get calls that say, "I didn't get a mint. Did I do something wrong? Did I not order enough?"'

"Then he explained how they came about. He came from the vending business, and when he started the helicopter company he had pallets of candy still around. So when the new company filled an order, they'd put in candy as a thank you. Later, when they ran out of candy, they bought mints. "

Yvonne stopped and asked me, "So was it the mints that made the brand?"

I got it. "No! Better and faster made the brand, and the mints became a symbol. People love the mints because they love the company, not the other way around."

That story made me understand where I'd been going wrong. My department had tried gimmicks, the equivalent of those mints—the giveaways and the cute posters and all the rest—but we hadn't figured out how to make a real connection with our internal customer, so our attempts at being playful remained just gimmicks. Although most of the people in the company would say that we were "nice" and "good presenters," we knew that most people hated coming to training classes and most didn't think they got much out of them. We had to figure out what we loved about Training and how to get them to love it in return.

We eventually figured that out, but I'm getting ahead of myself. First, let me get back to Yvonne and how, even as I was agreeing with her, she wasn't satisfied.

## The Hard/Kiss/Smart-Ass Choice

The conference room where we sat was one of those with a glass wall opening onto the hall, and a pair of co-workers passed by and made faces, knowing that I'd made fun of my prize, the coaching session. I turned my chair so I wouldn't be distracted.

Yvonne gave me the wary-eye and sighed. "Something's missing. You're understanding me and saying the right things, but I don't feel the energy. I haven't gotten through to you. Let's face it: You're not going to change."

I objected and swore that I was all-in, ready to transform my work, but she just played at looking beaten and, shrugging, said, "I can't figure out what's missing. There's something that's holding you back, some doubt that's shadowing our conversation."

(Much later I understood that she was goading me; she wasn't trying to get me to agree but to disagree. She was trying to get me to criticize her, or, rather, to get me to criticize her ideas and her plan for me.)

I didn't doubt her, I insisted. Eventually though, she got me to admit that while I believed her, I didn't believe I could be what she was describing. I just couldn't see myself as developing some special skill, and I sure couldn't see myself as a "hard-ass" and was pretty sure I didn't want to be one if I could.

# CHAPTER FOUR:
## The Magnificent Intolerance

She said lightly, joking (I think), "You haven't started and already you're back-sliding."

I gave her my adorably helpless look, and she turned steely, saying, "Look, there isn't a choice, remember? If you aren't going to be a hard-ass, you're going to be a kiss-ass. The only way to not be a commodity is to refuse to let people be ordinary, even when they dress it up as world class. You have to be the leader. The one with the heart and guts to say, NO! NOT GOOD ENOUGH! You have to be the one demanding greatness. It's that, or it's Inadvertent Mediocrity. Your choice."

What could I say?

Yvonne brushed something off her skirt before leaning forward and saying, "That brings me to the point about leadership being more than the old 'Hire good people and get out of the way.' Sounds great, but here's the question: If employees would do exactly what they do without you being around, what is your purpose?"

This time she didn't wait for me, but said, "There isn't one. But there is a *need* for leadership because of what we just talked about, how the default setting for a team is to be an imitation of other teams.

"Now, let's dig into Numbers Two and Three."

2. **Leadership is a magnificent intolerance.**

3. **Bureaucracy evolves; organizations devolve.**

She said, "Let me tell you about one man who went from 'liked' to' leader,' one who understands how to be an anti-bureaucrat."

She gave me another marvelous story, this one about an insurance agent in South Dakota. He's with one of the giant insurance companies and, despite being in small market, is one of the top ten agents in the country. Let me digress a little and give you some background because I've since met Terry and his is an example worth savoring.

## Find People Who Love Something

Terry Richter says his goal is to work 100 days a year. No, he isn't trying to cut back— he's trying to get UP to 100 days. That's because he's still working his way back from brain surgery eight years ago and tires quickly most days. However, he insists that his current success has come not just since his medical problems but BECAUSE of them. He was once a workaholic, a guilty one—"When I was at work I was thinking about my family, and when I was with my family I was thinking about work." He did well financially, but as he describes it, "God had to hit me across the back of the head with a 2X4 for me to let go and let the team do it."

That's starting to sound like the old advice on delegating, but he puts it differently...

---

"Instead of 'Hire good people and get out of the way,' it's *'Find people who love something and help them do it better. "*

"I have people who love to sell, but also people who love answering the phone, love detail, and so on.

"The secret is to get people doing what they love to do. All you do is ask, 'What do you want?' 'What's a good day?' and 'How much do you want to make?'"

~ TERRY RICHTER

---

That sounds good and it sounds easy—what it doesn't sound is "hard," but hold on. Most managers, especially in entrepreneurial offices, come to be mom to the office family, and that's how most managers stop leading and start helping, doing pieces of everyone else's job. It was Richter's medical problems that forced him to force the employees not to rely on him.

"Before," he explained, "I had one employee who would bring me her problems every afternoon before she left work. I would say 'I'll take care of it' and turn around and put the file on my credenza. One day I noticed that I had a foot-high pile of her work on my credenza, and every day when she went home her desk was completely clear."

The new Richter's approach: "When employees come to me with a problem, I tell them to come up with two solutions and then ask me which one I think is better. They stopped asking. They know that I'm not going to solve the problem for them, so they just do it themselves."

(Let me interrupt the story of Terry for a second to say that I've thought of that little example a hundred times since the day I met Yvonne. It wasn't just that I wanted to stop being "the helper" and start being the one getting helped; no, it was more than that—I went from helping employees do their jobs to helping them get better. Huge difference. Huge. Please take a minute, close your eyes, and think about that one before you go on. Slap.)

## Too Tough

Now we can get back to the story about Terry that Yvonne told me in the conference room. She said, "I should point out that just because you get employees doing what they say they love, it doesn't mean they'll be good at it. For instance, Terry had a young man out of college who thought he wanted to sell insurance, but the reality was that he wasn't a great sales-person and Terry couldn't get him to become one. Terry sat down with him and said this: 'If you were me, and you owned this agency, what would you do with you? The young sales-man replied, I would let me go.' And that's what happened.

"Once again, that doesn't sound 'hard,' does it? However, when I asked Terry if he would describe himself as 'demanding,' he shook his head and said, 'I have high expectations—high expectations for excellence.' But then, get this, he added, 'If you went to all the other agents in town and asked their employees, none would want to work for me. They would all say that I'm too tough.'"

Yvonne added, "Here's a guy who only works a couple of days a week, who is loved by his staff and who helps them to excel and do more than they thought possible, and yet, he insists that no other insurance employees who know his office would want to work for him. Why?"

That's when she passed along an example of what Terry means by "high expectations." One employee had a series of miseries in her personal life including a family member committing suicide and another being sent to prison. None of these were her fault, but they are tragedies that took time and energy. He said that he and the other employees had stepped in to help her reach her goals, but reaching them was still in doubt. When asked what would happen if the employee didn't meet her goals, he said, without hesitation, "We have a responsibility to our customers; if she can't do it, I have to get someone else."

"Okay," I told Yvonne, "now that's HARD. I don't think I could do that."

She shrugged with what might have been an ounce of understanding. She said, "But could you take an employee who dumps problems on you and give them the responsibility back? Can you say, 'That's an interesting problem, I'll be fascinated to see how you solve it'? Or, better yet, could you say, 'I know you can solve that; come up with three possible solutions and then come back and we'll talk them through'?"

I liked that. I smiled, picturing the response from the employees who'd grown lazy letting me handle all the trickiest parts of their jobs.

"And," she pressed on, "could you swap your old philosophy for Terry's and replace *'Hire good people and get out of the way,'* with *'Find people who love something and help them do it better'*?"

Oh, yes, I could. I liked the idea of seeking out people who *loved* some piece of our work, who could come up with a "cannibalistic butterfly" and delight in doing so. It would transform my hiring, but that was okay—if I hired excited people the energy would slosh around my department. And a leadership goal of "help them do better" certainly was more energizing than "get out of the way."

Yvonne pointed out that "help them do better" was another "hard" skill and we would cover it in a minute. But first, she needed to circle back. "Now, at last, now that we understand a little about Terry, I can let him bring these two principles to life." She tapped the paper at these two:

## 2. Leadership is a magnificent intolerance.

## 3. Bureaucracy evolves; organizations devolve.

Now, Terry as a case study of driving exceptional performance...

Terry Richter's agency has one receptionist and had grown to the point where they were getting more than 3,000 calls a month. This staff, especially the ear-weary receptionist, began lobbying for a second receptionist.

Instead of a "yes" or "no," Terry took some time to analyze the calls. The phone system recorded the calls in and out, so he was able to look at calling patterns. He discovered that there were more than 300 calls to the parent company's underwriters and nearly as many back. He knew that these calls were to get answers to questions that were available in materials in their offices. So he told his staff to stop making calls and start educating themselves by looking things up. He also asked the underwriters if they would respond to emails as quickly as phone calls. He says of them, "I'm their favorite person."

He also discovered that one employee had made and received 324 personal calls in the previous month. "She was fired," he explained, simply.

Terry also explored what it was that customers wanted when they called and learned that a considerable percentage of the calls were from customers who were asking for explanations of bills. For instance, if a customer added a new car to a policy and had been told that it would cost $45 a month, the first bill might come in at $65 because it covered a month and a half to catch up with the regular payments. So Terry and his staff made a point of anticipating customer questions and inoculating against them—for instance, telling people to expect the first bill to be larger and not to worry unless the *second* monthly invoice was too high.

The upshot? Terry said, "The next month we knocked off 1,800 calls." And of course by cutting the calls by more than half, discussion of a new receptionist was at an end.

Yvonne and I discussed the significance of that story and how it illustrated the point about bureaucracy—the natural "solution" to problems is to add more people or to add more rules. So I was clear on how bureaucracy evolves—we've all seen it, right? One important point of Terry's story is how a leader must be an anti-bureaucrat.

## The Other Bureaucracy

The more interesting of Yvonne's lessons was about organizations "devolving." The tendency is to cut corners, save time, be content with "good enough." After all, how often has someone at the office said to you, "It doesn't have to be anything special" or "Just take the proposal we did last time and change the names."

It isn't that people are lazy or inept; it's that we all are looking to be more efficient. And the result isn't "find people who love to do something and help them do it better"; it's "let's get this out of the way as fast as we can and move on to something else." Without anyone ever making the decision, the unspoken team standard is "good enough." Then, what's the overall definition of the team's "good enough"? *The weakest member of the team.* Everyone knows that's how good "good enough" is and tends to devolve to that level of performance. The weakest person defines acceptable every day when he turns up for work.

Yvonne said this, "That's where leadership comes in, not just giving permission and answering questions, but asking interesting questions like, 'How could we make it so customers don't need to call us about their bills?' What you are really asking is, 'How could we be better? How could we eliminate bureaucracy and get better at the same time?' THAT'S leadership."

I got it—I needed to stop helping the people who worked for me do their jobs and start helping them get better. I needed them to stop coming to me for answers and get them to start expecting hard questions. There was that word again—hard. Slap.

## The Positive Negative

Still, I looked down at the list, and there was that bit about leadership being a "magnificent intolerance." I told Yvonne that I didn't get it—that asking hard questions didn't seem to me to be the same as "intolerance." I told her that it seemed to me that she was going out of her way to state things in the negative.

This stopped her. She thought a long while and said, "Maybe that's the case. Without my realizing it, maybe I'm trying to counter all the happy-talk management. But I started emphasizing 'intolerance' after reading the work of consultant and statistician Davis Balestracci, who argues that organizational culture is largely defined by what you tolerate. If you're okay with missing deadlines but getting close, then that's the standard. If you're okay with setting low targets to make sure you hit them and then putting in a little padding, just in case, well, padding is the standard. So the line becomes, what you will and won't tolerate. To be great, you have to be intolerant:

*"You don't get what you want or what you need; you get what you refuse to accept less than."*

"We now have a workplace where virtually all employees were raised on positive reinforcement. The unintended consequence is systematic self-satisfaction. Managers get positive reinforcement from giving positive reinforcement, creating a spiral of self-congratulation. The result is feel-good management that, sadly, often translates to soft, slow management.

"The antidote is to shove the organization along another axis, the competitive-surprise-experimentation one. *The increase in performance in an organization is predictable: you get only as much as you demand.*"

Yvonne stopped to let me absorb that and smiled at a thought. "I have a client who complained that his employees weren't creative. I told him a variation of what I'm telling you, You don't get as much innovation as you want; you get as much as you won't tolerate less than. He insisted that you couldn't mandate creativity. But I got him to put in metrics. He has a minimum number of ideas and experiments and a minimum percentage of sales from products introduced in the last year. If you're in a division that doesn't hit the standard, you don't participate in bonuses."

That was the sort of thing that I, a mid-level manager in a national corporation, could never do...at least I didn't think so. (Yvonne was starting to make me want to get creative with the rules.) So I asked for ideas on how I could set higher standards. Naturally, this led to a story, or rather, this time, a series of shorter ones, each a profile of a manager who refused to be ordinary.

Yvonne began by recounting a conversation she had with Kenneth Roman, who was CEO of the big ad agency, Ogilvy & Mather, and wrote a book about the agency's founder, David Ogilvy, entitled *The King of Madison Avenue*. (It turns out that Ogilvy was the person she was describing when she first pulled out a quote about being feared in the best way.)

Roman described his first encounter with the agency's standards of excellence: Within a few months of starting work at the agency, he was called away from dinner by a phone call from one of the agency employees who was working on a two-page magazine ad. Roman was told that the pages were too far apart, leaving an eighth of an inch of extra white space between them. The problem could be easily remedied, but doing so would cost $300 for new printing plates. Roman describes what transpired:

"I agreed that the fix made sense but pointed out that this was not the main campaign, only a coupon ad, and this was just a test market. The change could be made later. 'And the client has already approved it,' I added.

"The reproving response was swift. 'David says [pause] it's never too late to improve an ad—even after the client has approved it.' 'Spend the 300 bucks,' I agreed. Like the Church, the agency had standards."

I've since read Roman's bio of David Ogilvy, and it's replete with instances of Ogilvy's standards lifting the organization. One former employee (this was Peter Mayle, who went on to become a best-selling author) recalled getting his ad copy returned by Ogilvy, heavily marked with red pencil including this bit of marginalia: "Quack-quack. Belles lettres. Omit."

On another occasion, when Ogilvy feared the entire agency's standards were slipping, he wrote a series of memos under the heading "Escape From Dullsville."

Yvonne described asking Roman if working for such a demanding legend meant that Ogilvy was "scary." He immediately insisted, "No! He was fun and he was funny."

Here's the conclusion, that earlier quote from Yvonne…

---

"He was charming... and demanding... a lovable tyrant. Like many of the best leaders, he was feared in the best way: the employees didn't fear HIM; they feared LETTING HIM DOWN, feared failing to live up to the reputation for exceptional work that he protected with a ferocity that would impress a tigress with a toothache."

---

Yvonne asked me if I could write "Quack-quack" in the margin of an employee's report. When I hesitated, unsure, she said, "We need to work on that. We'll come back to it when we get to 'the triplets of truthfulness.' But for now, let's stick with intolerance as a key to management. There were studies done by a pair of sociologists back in the 1980s—Wilson and Kelling were their names—that came to be known as the 'Broken Windows Theory.'"

(I'm going to summarize here, because at the mention of the word "sociologists" I can picture your eyes getting heavy. But if you aren't already familiar with the idea, I think you'll find this is kinda cool. Trust me.)

Yvonne went on to describe this idea that if a housing project has a single broken window, the entire area is in danger of rapid decline. Makes sense—you see a broken window patched up with cardboard and duct tape, and you tend to think, "Bad neighborhood."

Here are a couple of the experiments Wilson and Kelling did...

In one, the researchers put an envelope sticking out of a mailbox, making it obvious that there was money inside. They chose a location where the envelope could easily be stolen by a person passing by, and that's just what happened about one time in eight. Then, when the researchers added some litter on the ground around the mailbox, the number of people giving in to temptation doubled, to one in four.

Another time they went to an alley where customers of a shopping center parked bikes. While the bike owners were shopping, the researchers hung advertisements on the handlebars. Meanwhile, they'd taken away the nearby trash receptacles, so the bike owners had to either pocket the ad or throw it on the ground. About one-third chose to just throw the ad down. But when they painted graffiti on the alley wall, the number of people who littered more than doubled.

Yvonne and I had a good talk about that second study. People saw that the alley wasn't being kept up, and they made a decision. However, we were guessing that they didn't really think about it, that they didn't stand there making calculations; no, they just threw down the ad and rode off.

———————

So, at some level, *the environment made the decision, not the person.* The message is this: You cut one lousy corner and you're a corner-cutter.

———————

I later saw a version of this principle in action with the not-so-lovable Steve Jobs of Apple. It was a *Fast Company* interview with Mark Parker, who was talking about meeting Jobs shortly after becoming CEO of Nike. He asked Jobs if he had any advice and Jobs replied, "Nike makes some of the best product in the world, product you lust after, absolutely beautiful, stunning product. But you also make a lot of crap. Just get rid of the crappy stuff and focus on the good stuff."

The Nike CEO said he expected Jobs to pause and then give a laugh to let him know he was kidding, but Parker reported, "There was a pause and *no* laugh."

Good line from Jobs, and there has never been a better example of the principle of magnificent intolerance than his work; still, Nike is a highly successful company, so it remains to be seen if the "crappy stuff" will pull down their reputation over time.

However, when it comes to management, I think the magnificent intolerance is absolute.

------

*Be very careful when you "look the other way." Your weakest employee is an announcement to your team and everyone the team works with, THIS LEVEL OF PERSON IS ACCEPTABLE TO ME. Your weakest output tells the world, THIS LEVEL OF PERFORMANCE IS ACCEPTABLE TO ME.*

*Just because you "looked the other way" doesn't mean everyone else doesn't see exactly where your minimum standard resides. It defines you. You are your weakest work.*

------

Yvonne added, "You can picture someone saying about your team, 'They have some great people, although they have that one guy who just doesn't get it—it makes you wonder.' And instead of talking about how good you are, they are worrying about your standards." Ouch.

## *He's* An Intolerant Hard-Ass?

Next, Yvonne pulled out her computer and showed me a video clip. She started by saying, "I know you're afraid to be thought of as a hard-ass, but that doesn't mean being some sort of macho bully. So I want to show you a bit of hard management in action, and who it is will surprise you."

Boy, did it. She fires up this video clip, and it's from the documentary *This is It* about, of all people, Michael Jackson. He's been called a lot of things, but I wouldn't have guessed that anyone would call him a hard-ass. When I said as much to Yvonne, she said, "That's because we didn't get to see him at work until this film showed him behind the scenes, getting ready for the national tour that never happened."

I wasn't eager to take career advice from Michael Jackson; after all, his personal life was bizarre and misguided, and I suppose that we could say it killed him. But Yvonne had pulled together some clips that showed him in rehearsal, and I had to admit that he was a master at work—not just a master performer, but manager.

First, he was conscious of creating something special and made everyone else fully conscious of it, too. There was never a "good enough" moment. Indeed, we get to watch as a choreographer and dancers have a lively exchange on how to properly do a crotch-grab during one dance number, and the choreographer, without irony, explains how the ballet dancer Baryshnikov would have done it. What? But that's the plane they believed they were on, creating art, even with the crotch-grab.

The scene that got Yvonne really worked up was Jackson with his Musical Director, who plays him a bit of a song and Jackson says flatly, "Pretty good. Pretty good." Bang. That idea is dead. "Pretty good" was all it took for it to be tossed out. Then the Music Director offers a new variation, and they experiment till it's just right.

Yvonne loved that exchange because it showed how "pretty good" can be an insult. It's as if the team leader had said, "It's good enough for other people, but not us." And the team believes it, without question or apology. We see the same spirit when the pyrotechnics guy demonstrates the fireworks above the stage, and the Director says, "Can we do that, times ten?" and the answer is, with delight, "Absolutely."

Yvonne said of that moment, "It would be easy for the fireworks tech to say, 'Hey, that's what's in the specs' or, bigger picture, to say, 'Hey, it's *just* a pop music concert.' That would be as easy as telling Steve Jobs, 'Relax, it's just a computer.'" She summarized it this way...

---

What I've seen in the best workplaces is a culture where the work is NOT about the audience/market/customers; it's about taking talent and taking off with it, luring it into the unknown, playing with the extraordinary for the sheer joy of being part of something *better than it has to be.*

"And that's exactly what elevates the best business endeavors, the joy of exploration into the frontier—better than it has to be.

"Isn't that what great employees want to experience, even if they don't know it yet?"

---

That left me a bit stunned. The truth is that I'd been a "good enough" kind of manager, a skilled corner-cutter, taking pride in being efficient. I had never considered "the joy of exploration" or "luring talent into the unknown," and while it seems crazy, *I had to admit it appealed to something deep in me, some all-but-forgotten urge to do something special, to rediscover the urge to create something that was better than it had to be, and to take my best employees there with me.*

Yvonne broke into my reverie and asked, playing with me, if I thought I could be as macho as Michael Jackson. Haha. But I got her point. Being "hard" wasn't about style, but standards. Maybe I could have a soft style and still have hard standards. Possible? I asked her, and she actually smiled and said, "If you can get your team to stop and smell the...." Here she paused and my mind inserted the word "roses." But no, she completed the sentence not with roses, but with "fish." Yeah, *fish*.

# CHAPTER FIVE:
## Smelling the Fish

Some people showed up to use the conference room, and we got booted. So we decided to head to the employee cafeteria. We'd talked through the lunch hour, into early afternoon, and it occurred to us both that we were hungry. We got sandwiches and found a corner where we could focus.

I'd brought along my note pad and the handwritten list, which she pointed to with her Diet Coke and said, "Time to review Numbers Four, Five, and Six—the Triplets of Truthfulness."

4. **Criticism is a compliment.**

5. **Never trust a manager who loves everything you do.**

6. **Stop and smell the roses, yes, but sometimes you've got to stop and smell the fish.**

"All morning we've been talking about why being 'hard' is critical. Now we get to talk about how to be hard and do it in a way that's winning rather than off-putting. Here's where we've really got work to do."

Not unkindly she added, "This is the point where, watching you this morning with your employees, I wanted to barf into your wastebasket." She examined my face for a reaction. I smiled. She smiled. "So you're not offended?"

"Not really. It's like those stories of the Zen master whacking students with a stick."

"I've never thought of myself as whacking people with a stick, but maybe that's what it is—most organizations are all carrot and no stick. Why do you suppose that is?"

I knew she was testing me, and I tried to come through, making a list—

1. an emphasis on positive reinforcement, as in "catch someone doing something right,"
2. the unwillingness to hurt someone's feelings,
3. a desire to be liked and be a "good guy," and
4. people tend to live up to expectations, so by assuming the best, you are more likely to get the best.

Not bad. That was so fine a list I was winning myself back to the notion of positive management.

Yvonne waited me out and then said, "Excellent list. It's easy to see why managers would want to be cheerleaders, right? But we already know the other list: the commodity-product trap, the devolution of organizations, the fallacy of trying to be world class, and once you start choosing easy conversations, pretty soon you're refusing to see what's wrong. "

She was getting worked up, leaning toward me and gesturing with her sandwich. "Here's my best example. There's a consultant who works with doctors' offices round the country. She's also named Yvonne—Yvonne Mart Fox of Middleton, Wisconsin—and she comes in and does the tough work that doctors are too weak to do.

"One of Fox's assignments was to come into a practice where the lead doctor suspected that someone was embezzling. She came in, pretending to do an efficiency study, and eventually identified the culprit. When she found out who it was, she called the man in charge, the one who hired her to solve the mystery, but he refused to take the calls and eventually told her that he didn't want to know, that he couldn't handle the truth. That's how soft some mangers become. An extreme example, true, but it tells the story of how people can refuse to face up to negatives."

Sure, that was extreme and I understood the point, but I objected to the bigger point, that she was ignoring the advantages of being positive. I was still thinking my list had some solid logic behind it, and said as much.

She replied and told me...

———————

"I'm not asking you to turn negative. No, no, no. I want you to be your team's biggest fan. I want you to believe in your team so much that you refuse to let them fall into accidental mediocrity. That takes more than praise; it takes challenge and daring and the willingness to reject the ordinary and that will come down to you—YOU!—saying the equivalent of NOT GOOD ENOUGH.  That doesn't mean saying, 'You stink,' but it might mean writing 'Quack-quack' in the margin or saying, 'pretty good' in a way that says, 'It's okay, but I was hoping for better.' This means *getting yourself and you team comfortable with high expectations.*"

———————

Maybe I showed my doubt because she turned harder. "It's time for me to give you a compliment, by which I mean, a criticism. You've let yourself get soft. Watching you today I could tell that you were trying to manipulate people by complimenting them rather than telling them to be better."

"I was catching them doing something right." I gave a winning half-smile to let her know that I was joking.

With a nod, she acknowledged the change in tone and said, kindly, "We need to get you to make friends with criticism, giving and getting. Which is hard because we live in an age of anti-criticism."

This brought back some of my training about how to handle a situation where you wanted to criticize an employee. "I was taught in one seminar that if I was going to criticize anyone I should make sure to give a compliment first, then the criticism, and then another compliment. The guy sitting next to me at that seminar leaned over and said, 'Sounds like a shit sandwich to me.'"

It was the first time I'd seen Yvonne laugh, and she was no lady about it, tossing in a bit of snort.

"And the sad thing is that it won't work," she remarked. "I've seen people pump up the compliments and then dance so lightly over the criticism that the person misses the point, leaving with the idea that he's doing fine and nothing needs to change. Or, if they hear the criticism, that's all they're going to hear anyway, and the compliments just make them resent the criticism. Hopeless. That's why I believe in announcing that you want to have a hard conversation and zero-in on what needs to be different. That's why I love that expression about smelling the fish."

## Smelling the Fish

Yvonne explained that the statement came to her when she was frustrated that her employees were being so polite and positive that they avoided the negative. She kept saying, "We need to face facts," but failed to break through the cone of positivism. Then, one day she blurted out to her team, "We keep stopping to smell the roses and that's great, *but now it's time to stop and smell the fish!*" What?

She wasn't sure how that popped into her mind—perhaps she heard the expression "put the fish on the table," which is used by a Swiss professor and hostage negotiator, George Kohlrieser, to describe conflict management. (Kohlrieser was helping some fishermen clean fish when it occurred to him that what they were doing was a metaphor for dealing with conflict—before you could have a nice fish dinner you had to put the thing on the cleaning table and make a bloody mess.)

When Yvonne told her team "to stop and smell the fish," there was something about it that was surprising and funny and funky, and it charmed the team brain out of its typical thought patterns. The team began to really *talk*, to really consider what smelled; that is, to discuss their weaknesses, especially when it came to knowing their customers.

Here's how Yvonne summed up what smelling the fish could accomplish...

---

"In most good organizations, managers have gotten good at stopping to smell the roses; that is, to notice what's going well and recognize those responsible. But we also need to take time and stop to smell the fish, to figure out what isn't going well, to identify what stinks and deal with it."

---

Yvonne brought the message home, saying, "Now, imagine if you started using that little statement about stopping to smell the fish. It makes people smile. It disarms them. It isn't scary like 'face up to what's wrong.' Smelling the fish is a lively way of saying, 'Let's get serious about getting better.' That isn't scary; it's energizing. At one company I was with it got to the point where, when one executive was introducing me to another, he said in a way that lets me know this is high praise, 'He's someone who really knows how to smell the fish.'"

This struck me as strange, but as Yvonne said that last sentence, I found myself yearning to be that guy, the one who could speak hard truths in a way that people welcomed the conversation. I wanted to be a guy who got his team to stop for roses *and* for fishes.

Even as I was thinking that, Yvonne was pressing ahead, saying, "Okay, so what are these fish that we want to pass around and let everyone smell?"

"The facts," I replied. "Not just the good ones but the unpleasant ones that people would rather not deal with."

"Yes, the fish are the facts. We have to have the facts. We need metrics. There's that old line, 'What gets measured gets done,' and it works. In the case of this executive I've been talking about, he loved to talk about numbers—the percent of time in the field and how many days since employees had talked to customers. If the leader can cite those numbers, I bet every manager can. That's how metrics shape the company. So I want to spend some time on them, but I'd like to hold off a few minutes and review the remaining two triplets. Is that good?"

Naturally, I agreed, and Yvonne tapped the page again…

## 4. Criticism is a compliment.

## 5. Never trust a manager who loves everything you do.

Here's some of what she next told me…

"What is the absolute easiest response to an employee's work? The one thing that they always agree with and takes the least time to prepare and the least follow-up? It's 'Great work.' You say that to someone, and they never disagree, never argue, never say, 'What do you mean?' and never make excuses or offer explanations. It's fast and easy, and that's why it's overdone.

"Add in those other things we talked about, like believing in positive reinforcement and being liked, and you have the perfect formula for happy mediocrity."

I interrupted here to remind her that we'd had this conversation by saying, "Applauding the potty."

"Exactly. When you take the time to criticize, THAT'S the real compliment. Why? Think of the underlying message you're sending to the person you're talking to:

- I think enough of you that I'm willing to take my time to truly analyze your work and really pay attention.
- I believe you can get better, that I see you as improving and growing in your work and career.
- I care about you and your contribution to the team.

Those are *real compliments,* and you know they are real because you are going to back them up with genuine thought, attention, and effort. The other compliments, the 'great work' ones, are easy, and you can't be sure they're true because they are unbacked, no gold in them, just words.

"Now, flip it, and let's consider the underlying message from the boss who always praises everything an employee does. It either means that such a boss…

- Doesn't care enough to take the time and attention to help the employee improve, or
- Is too wimpy or self-centered to offer help, or
- Doesn't know how to help the person improve.

"What the ever-praised employees should conclude is that the boss has nothing to teach them or doesn't care enough to bother. This means they should seek out a better boss or at least find mentors to do what the boss can't. *Great employees* want to be challenged, to have new and intriguing assignments."

Then with a sly smile, Yvonne added this aside, "What do non-great employees want?" Before I could come up with an answer, she said, "Who cares?"

Next, she gave me an example of what can happen when you get a boss who has nothing to offer but compliments. (Think about that last phrase: nothing to offer but compliments. Slap.)

> She'd met a guy named Steve Gavatorta, who's now a speaker and sales trainer, but who was reminiscing about his days as a young sales guy. He went from college to one of the giant consumer products companies selling to retailers. Although he was a solid prospect as a sales guy, his boss didn't know what to

do with him, so Gavatorta struggled, untrained and un-led. Because the boss was what Gavatorta called "an attaboy manager," it never occurred to him how poorly he was doing. Then, one day, he accidentally got the truth.

Another manager, not his boss, went with him on his rounds one day and wrote up a summary of woeful impressions, then sent it to Gavatorta by mistake.

Reading that report, his first real analysis of his performance, and unaccustomed to taking criticism as a compliment, Gavatorta was shell-shocked. He said that after reading the report, he had to go lie down, and once he did, he began thinking, "This is my first job, and I'm going to get fired. I'll go back home a failure and go to work in my father's produce shop. This is the lowest day of my life."

But rather than crawl home, he decided to take a shot at changing companies, even taking the odd step of asking an executive at his current employer to write a recommendation. That executive agreed, but then made a call and got Gavatorta transferred—to work for the man who'd written the scathing report.

Punishment? Just the opposite. The new manager was a teacher/coach, one who taught Gavatorta to sell and about whom he says, "He turned my career around in a matter of months, and I worked for the company another ten years. He taught me the fundamentals— he passed a skill set to me that I still use and teach to others."

Yvonne summed up that story by saying, "Notice that the turnaround happened on what he thought was the worst day of his life. It was actually the best day of his career because he'd found a boss who was wiling and able to tell him what he was doing wrong and how to fix it."

I wondered aloud how his first boss, the lousy one, had gotten in that position and stayed there. But Yvonne didn't share my doubt, shrugging it off. Then she said...

---

"There are plenty of bosses who let people fail, blame the employee, and hire someone else. But leadership is not about getting rid of employees—any idiot can throw away assets—it's about making people better, about teaching and training and even about saving them. Leadership is creating a better future for the company by creating better employees."

---

Then she went on to tell me tales of someone she described as the "ultimate employee-turnaround specialist," Jenny Lang, who managed a highly successful automobile dealership in Scottsdale until her recent promotion to COO of a dealership group.

Yvonne described her as an "effervescent five-foot-one," which must make her one of the smallest auto executives in the country. Proud of being outspoken and fearless about it, she frequently quotes her mother as saying, "You can say anything you want, to anybody, as long as you say it with respect."

Yvonne admires Lang so much that she's started a collection of her sayings, and she sent these to me...

# THE INIMITABLE JENNY LANG

- Girlfriends don't call me because they want to hear, "Oh yeah, you're right." No, they call me because they know that if they're making a mistake I'm going to say, "That's bullshit." I had one friend recently tell me "You're the one person who I know will tell me the truth."

- Once you go into victim mode, you no longer have control over yourself or your world.

- I tell my employees who aren't thriving in their jobs, "You wouldn't want me not to deal decisively with underperformance."

- My mother was a schoolteacher, and everything was a lesson. My sisters and I used to joke about this, saying, "Does everything have to be a lesson? But my mother gave me advice that I still remember, including "Life isn't for the weak," and when I got married, "There'll be times you'll hate your husband—it will pass."

- So many of my employees have been promoted into other jobs in other dealerships that I think of my employees as being "on loan to me."

- I'm very aware of energy levels, and when I walk into someone's office I can feel their energy. Sometimes I'll say to them, "You've got weird energy—what's going on? They might say "Nothing." But if I persist, saying "No, I can feel it," that's when they often open up.

- *People need to know you can get angry—that's a tool in the toolkit.*

Is there any doubt that this is a woman who can really get people to stop and smell the fishes? The day I met with

Yvonne, she singled Jenny out as her best role model for making dramatic increases in employee performance. Take a look at this example, one Jenny sent Yvonne, so it's in her own words...

*I had this young girl who had started with the company seven years ago at the ripe young age of seventeen. During these years, as my job duties and titles changed, hers seemed to be parallel to mine. I recognized potential in her and took her under my wing.*

*As you get used to working for someone, sometimes you get too comfortable. She began to experience what I call "job rot." She was too comfortable, too long. Her work ethic began to wane. I had several conversations with her regarding this. I always ask my employees in these types of situations, once we agree that there is an issue, what they are going to do differently and when will they start. All conversations seemed to have fallen on deaf ears.*

*I was paying her a more than fair wage, and I felt I was not getting my money's worth. I then brought her in, cut her pay $3 an hour, wrote her up, and put her on notice. I suggested that she had job rot, and maybe it was time she left the company, as she was clearly taking advantage of a long-term relationship with myself as her boss.*

*I told her she could handle this situation one of two ways. She could either be a victim and blame others and learn nothing, or she could rise above, take ownership, and make this a turning point in her career. I told her the outcome was directly her choice. And in the end, if she was fired, it was by her doing, not mine.*

*To my delight, she turned 180 degrees and completely*

The 12 Laws of Driving Exceptional Performance

*plugged in, appreciated her job and those around her, and began to excel. Months later, when I was approached by another manager as to her potential in another position within the company, I gladly recommended her. She took the position and to date is excelling in a position that has more than doubled her income.*

Yvonne and I analyzed that example at length. There's so much there to admire. First, can you imagine cutting someone's pay, saying you aren't getting your money's worth? I couldn't. But somehow Jenny pulled it off. And how she did it is a device she frequently employs: In her difficult conversations with employees, she always explains to them that it is a *"fork in the road,"* and then projects what happens down each path. One path is "You blame me. Then you'll get resentful and will have more problems. Is that what you want?" Then the other path: "This can be a turning point and..." followed by an alternative future, an upward spiral of success.

Brilliant, no?

For Jenny, it all flows from that advice from her mother, "You can say anything you want, to anybody, as long as you say it with respect." Hearing how she operates, you get a good working workplace definition of "respect" —it's assuming the best about the other person's motives. As Lang puts it, "Going into any interaction with an employee or peer, I establish with that person and myself what the *end result* needs to be. If you do that, you can understand each other and create an environment where you exchange ideas. Then we can figure out what we'll do differently."

"Notice," Yvonne said, "how it's all about the end result and what we'll do differently. I love that 'we'll.' That's what moves criticism to another plane, to helping and learning."

With that, Yvonne stood, did a stretch, and suggested we leave the cafeteria and walk around the building's courtyard. "We need to talk about the right criticism to the right person at the right time."

## Transforming Criticisms to Compliments

As we walked, Yvonne said, "Whenever I'm entering a conversation about criticism, I like to start with a review of the art of turning analysis into action. You need to go into the conversation hyper-aware of emotional energy. Criticism has massive emotional content, and it can easily go negative or positive—think of it as a rocker switch and we want to make sure it goes to the positive. That's what I love about starting the conversation by 'smelling the fish" and 'criticism is a compliment.' I like to start there—to set the expectation that the conversation is about getting better, about succeeding. I want to remove the fear, anger, and resentment and get to what matters—getting better."

Surprised, I pulled a face and said, "Looking at the woman you chose as the master of the tough conversation, I'd say that Jenny Lang used fear and anger in her 'choose the path' conversations. I mean, she cut that one woman's pay. That's not much of a compliment."

"Good point, and that's why we're having this part of the conversation—I don't want you going around insulting people. You don't inspire people by telling them how terrible they are."

I thought of her telling me she wanted to barf in my waste-basket, but let it slide.

"In Jenny's case, she has established a culture of challenge and blunt conversation, and, remember, she was clear, right from the start, that the employee had the choice—*two* paths." (Here I remembered how Yvonne had given me a choice when she started analyzing my work—soft or hard.) "And also this was a case where Jenny was dealing with job rot and employees who were underperforming, so those were change-or-leave conversations. That's a rare conversation, maybe you'll have one or two a year. I'm talking about good people getting better. I love that book title *Good to Great;* that was about corporations, but the same jump applies to individuals."

I nodded. Still, the two paths had a bit of the old "show them the instruments of torture" about it, so I continued to believe that the two paths were carrot-and-stick.

Yvonne pressed on, again pointing to the list she'd given me, explaining a principle that has been one I've come back to many times:

## 7. They ALWAYS KNOW.

She said, "One of the reasons to adopt the Triplets of Truth-fulness is that the truth makes you more effective. I believe that we all have built-in lie detectors and that we connect on levels other than mere conscious thought. I won't go into this because you'll probably think I'm crazy, but we all have energy fields and I believe that part of our evolution, our survival, is to sense the energy of others. Go ahead, make a joke—I'm used to it."

I shrugged. I was agnostic on the whole vibrations/chemistry/body language subject.

"Most people, especially men, think it's ridiculous, but there's research."

(Another warning of "Danger: Sociology Ahead!" is in order. Yvonne loves research because she likes putting numbers to ideas. I get that. Still, I'll cut this part short because I don't want to lose you when we've still got important work to do.)

Yvonne said, "One study that I find fascinating involved participants who each watched one of four videos of a leader giving feedback. Two of the four videos were positive feedback and two negative. Then, within each pair, the person playing the leader was supposed to show facial expressions that were, in the researchers terms, congruent or incongruent. You follow?"

"Sure. You're saying that one video showed positive feedback with a positive boss, and one positive feedback with a negative boss. Then the same pair for the two negative feedback bosses."

"Exactly. Then the participants rated the bosses. The worst rating was the positive feedback with the negative expressions."

This made sense to me. "People don't want to deal with the mixed message. The word 'weasel' springs to mind."

"Yes. And no one wants to work for a weasel, even one who's saying nice things. Maybe we could even say especially one saying nice things. Plus, there's a body of research around what's called 'mood contagion.' People pick up the mood of others around them, especially the boss. So that would lead us back to the positive Mr. Smiley boss. But, if you buy in, even a little, to the notion that people sense what you're really thinking, then you have to build a team that lets you be happy and mean it."

That brought back a memory. "I once worked for a man who often said to the team, 'Make me proud,' and we really wanted to. His reaction was like a scoreboard. He wasn't easy to please, but if we worked hard, we could make him proud and that was a victory we all shared in."

"There's one piece of mood-contagion research that I don't usually talk about because it would be easy to misuse, but I think you need to know this. One study looked at the effort groups put in on a task, and the group worked harder for a boss in a bad mood than one in a good mood."

"I can see that."

"And can you see how easy it would be to wear out the bad-mood strategy?"

I did—if a boss is always in a bad mood, you'd just start avoiding him or her. Then it hit me—Slap— "On the other hand, if the boss is always in a good mood, always positive and delighted with everything you do, you take that boss for granted. You get bored playing a video game you always win. Now I understand why Jenny Lang said that anger was a tool in her toolkit."

She nodded slightly, pleased with a slow student. "Good. So the first part of the transforming criticisms to compliments is congruence—make it true because they are going to know anyway. Just assume that the other person can read your thoughts. Assume that They ALWAYS KNOW."

Although I was glowing with new knowledge, I had a sudden objection—I had known plenty of clueless people, ones who couldn't take a hint much less figure out my unspoken thoughts. I challenged her and this was her response...

---

"The assumption that they ALWAYS KNOW is for your sake, not theirs. It keeps you from being lazy with your words and your face. You will develop an honest face because you're forcing yourself to be an honest person, one who wants the best for the other person and for the team. It's mental discipline. It's for you and your face, not for them."

---

## The Wrong Way

Yvonne pressed ahead. "Another of the inspiring bosses I've met is Holly Dance, with Prometric, a company that does testing all over the world—things like the CPA exam—millions of tests a year. Holly is in charge of their customer service, all the employees who interact with the test-takers. Holly is a star within the company. The time I met her she had just won two of the company's highest awards, something no one else had done. She is also the most articulate leader I've met on the subject of criticism and how to do it right.

"When I talked with her, she gave me examples of the times in her career when she got the wrong type of criticism, and you won't be surprised that her very first example was hearing this comment from one old boss: 'You're doing great—what more can I say?'

"Just remembering that comment brought back Holly's frustration; you could sense how she'd lost respect for that boss. She recounted her thought process: 'What more can I say?' *'Lots! Where can I grow? What are my towering strengths that I can make even stronger? Do I have any fatal flaws? Am I ready for a stretch assignment? What opportunities in the greater company are out there for me?'*

"That's how great employees think—they want to be challenged, to grow and evolve, not be patted on the head."

Yvonne then related two other criticisms that had annoyed Holly rather than helped her, along with her reactions:

"I don't really see your role adding value to the business."

*What do you mean by this? Is it me? Is it my role?*

"Maybe you will fail at this project."

*What am I supposed to do with that? How about saying instead, "How can I help you succeed in this project?" or "In order to succeed in this project, what things do you think need to change immediately?"*

"What can we make of those failed criticisms?" Yvonne asked me.

"That insults are useless."

"Yes, they lack the 'critique' in criticism. The word critique implies the thought and analysis that's missing in an insult. Insults raise a lot of questions without giving any guidance. They are the wrong path without a discussion of the right path."

## The Critique

"So," she continued, "our analysis is always results-oriented and... What?"

She had some supernatural ability to sense when I was mentally disagreeing with her. I confessed, "I wasn't going to interrupt, but I am confused by something that just popped into my mind. I liked it when the ad guy wrote 'Quack-quack' in the margin of ad copy. But he didn't rewrite the sentence, did he? And didn't we conclude before that the worst boss is one who does everything for the employee and that the best boss makes the employee come up with solutions. So, doesn't that make 'the right path' the same thing as telling them what to do?"

"Thank you for objecting," she began, and I could tell she meant it. I was used to keeping my doubts to myself, and she would have none of that. "My fault. I'm covering a lot of ground in a rush, and I should have made distinctions. Yes, David Ogilvy's 'quack' was a crack, just a shot. He had established a culture where he could playfully tell someone that an ad seemed weak to him. It was a challenge to the writer to go back and do better. He could have written, 'I think this could use a bit more work' or some such, but the 'quack' was quick and lively—it showed the creativity Ogilvy wanted in response. And all of this is employee specific—I'll bet he knew that the employee would take 'quack' as a challenge and turn what was a weak section of the ad into a great one. Then, as for Jenny Lang and her two paths, we already talked about how her examples were failing employees. And her path isn't do-this-and-that, it's about getting employees to reconsider how they work. She was showing them how good things could be."

Yvonne continued, saying, "I read that Barry Sonnenfeld, the filmmaker, puts 'DB' in the margin of scripts. It stands for Do Better. I can picture a scriptwriter getting back a script and boasting to her husband, 'It only had three DBs—a new record!' So it could be a scorecard and an efficient way for Sonnenfeld to lift performance. Remember, what counts is *the emotional energy*. THEY ALWAYS KNOW. In this case, what they know is his intent—was he making them raise their standards and was he helping them make a better movie? They would know. And when they do, the criticism doesn't have to be a big-deal conversation."

She stared off for an instant, remembering, then went on to tell me about John Genzale, who'd been a newspaper editor and was now teaching part-time at Columbia and living in Italy the rest of the time, starting a new team in the Italian

Baseball League. She spoke with admiration, saying, "This is a man who loves baseball, Italy, and teaching and who has found a way to combine all three into a career. He is one tough boss, lovably demanding. And he told me a story from his newspaper days about working with a young woman he thought was highly skilled, but had some weaknesses in her writing.

This young writer had an inability to put into her stories what journalists call a 'peg,' a paragraph early in a story that gives it context. I'm not sure I understand what John means by a peg, but apparently it was a major shortcoming in the work of this woman. Being a born educator, he'd explained and explained. Finally, one day in his office he was reading one of her stories and...no peg. She shrugged and said that she kept forgetting. In exasperation, he stood and grabbed a big felt-tip marker off his desk and wrote on the wall in giant letters the word PEG.

She never again gave him a story without a peg. By the way, when John's boss complained that he'd have to get someone to paint over the word, John said no, let it stay. And it did, for the rest of his time there. I suspect that the entire staff became peg geniuses."

Yvonne asked my opinion of that example, and I told her that I understood that, done right, it was lively and playful, and it certainly was memorable. On the other hand, the writer could have found it insulting or embarrassing, especially if he told people why there was a giant word PEG on his wall.

"Just so. I know John well, and people who've worked for him tell Genzale stories and that's part of his impact on people. I don't doubt that there are people who disliked working for

John, but I know that anyone who worked for him believed that he wanted to build a great organization and wanted them to excel. If that drives off some people, well..."

She let that hang, giving me time to realize this...

---

If I could develop a reputation as a lively, playful boss, one who was famous for high expectations, what sort of people would want to work on my team?

Yeah. Exactly.

---

## Just When I Thought I Was There

With each example Yvonne gave me, I could feel myself getting mentally tougher, getting to the point where I could see myself pulling off hard leadership. But each time I thought I was almost there, she had a way of letting me know I had further to go. Get this example (I'm paraphrasing Yvonne here)...

Matt Prunier leads a sales team for Northwestern Mutual, one of the big life insurance companies. He had a new employee who'd been a top performing rookie, but who had had suddenly lost momentum, and his sales had dropped off.

Matt sat him down for an extraordinary fish-smelling session. He invited the young sales guy to picture himself going to the mall and sitting and watching people pass by for several hours. He asked him, "I want you to be judgmental. I want you to watch the fathers and to tell me which ones seem like good dads. Picturing yourself doing that, what percentage do you think would you see actively being good fathers?" He wasn't sure and said "Not many."

Then he repeated that exercise, this time judging the men on being good husbands and spouses.

As I repeat that story, I'm not sure that even now I can tell you the point of that exercise, except to get the young guy in some sort of zone of critical analysis. Then Matt turned that analysis on him...

"I remember that in your interview for this job, you said that your father and grandfather were your heroes and role models and that you wanted to be like them. Right?"

He agreed.

"Then you're being a hypocrite."

The young guy objected, confused. Matt added, "Have you lived up to the person your father and grandfather would want you to be?"

Naturally, the kid got frosty at this. He argued that it was wrong to talk about his family and eventually got furious and walked out of the meeting.

BUT, he returned to Matt's office that afternoon, barked "THERE!" as he slapped down a list of seven new appointments with prospects, then walked back out.

In Matt's words, "That conversation turned him around. He's been killing it ever since."

I don't know about you, but that was too much for me. Yvonne, however, merely gave a shrug and an inverted smile, then said, "The reason it worked is because Matt knew this kid, knew what buttons to push."

"But it's just so personal."

"No. It was a reminder of the young man's own definition of himself and his greatness. He was angry that he'd misplaced himself."

"Yes, I get that, but in defining 'hard' for myself, I have to put that one over my personal line."

"That's fine. I understand. But, if you were in Matt's place and you let that young employee go on being mediocre and eventually fail, who's the one being kind? You or Matt?" Slap.

## Who Seeks Out Criticism?

Before Yvonne let go of the topic of transformative criticism, she brought up the other side—how difficult it was to get helpful critiques of one's work. She began with, "Who seeks out criticism? [pause] Only people who want to get better."

That took us back to the point about people being commodity products and not knowing it. If you don't get honest appraisals against the highest standards, you settle into a self-satisfied routine and never get to see what you could be and have. If all you're getting is high praise, you might just be like the student who always gets an A+ so decides to do a little less because a plain old A is just fine. But getting the right criticism at the right time isn't easy. You solve that problem by seeking out frequent critiques.

"Let me tell you about Angie Hicks," Yvonne said. "She's the Angie in Angie's List, the internet company that rates local service providers like landscapers and doctors." I gave a look that told her I knew about the company.

"I was going to talk with her, so I went to her blog to prepare and I found this note: 'If you're in the Columbus, Ohio, area, stop by Cup o' Joe in German Village tomorrow between 1:00 and 2:30 for a cup of coffee and a chat. I'll be waiting!'

"When I spoke with Angie, I asked about that little invitation and she explained that she has such meetings three or four times a year, in different cities, usually in coffee shops, and that all local members receive an email invitation. This is a chance to meet customers and know them better, but she also goes hoping to hear about problems. The best business-people understand that complaints are an opportunity, the entrepreneurial equivalent of 'criticism is a compliment.'

"For instance, one member somewhere in the Midwest told Angie that she was caring for her elderly parents in Florida and wanted the company's rating of services in that city, but didn't want to have to pay for a second membership in Florida. So Angie went back and developed an option for members to add a city, at a discounted rate. I'm sure there were people with second homes, or whatever, who saw the discount and thought, 'What a great idea—I never thought of adding another city.'"

As was her way, Yvonne wanted to back up and discuss what the example had to teach us. "Was that member complaining?" she asked.

"Sure. At least that's how she thought of it."

"Agreed. But that's not what the wise executive hears.

*A complaint is a present in homely wrapping paper. Tear off the wrapping, and there's money inside.*"

Then we began to consider how someone in my position could get more useful criticism. After all, I worked at company with a culture of politeness, and most of my colleagues were people who'd been raised in the same "we're all above average" mindset.

Yvonne suggested going to five colleagues and saying, "I'm trying to up my game. I'd like to set up a time to talk and ask you for suggestions on how I could get better."

(Later, I tried it. Four of the five just buttered me up like a tub of popcorn. Only one made an effort, and it was mostly generic comments. So I tried again with five more, and again. It took me fifteen people to find two I could count on to tell me the truth. Neither worked in my company. And both, by the way, have had terrific success in their fields and have eagerly asked me to return the favor.)

From Yvonne I learned that saying "Any feedback?" is taken as request for praise, like a dog sticking his head under your hand, wanting to be petted. Instead, you have to ask questions like, "Who's your favorite supplier (or sales rep or customer), and what makes them special?" or "Can you show me a report that you thought was really first-rate?" Doing so takes positivism and turns it into a critique. Just remember that what you get are the equivalent of best practices—you don't get them to imitate, but to keep up as you look for ways to surpass.

# Metrics—The Automatic Good Cop/Bad Cop

(OK, here it comes. I have to warn you upfront that this is about measuring performance, so it's about numbers and I know some of you really, really *hate* talking numbers. So, if this part bogs down for you, well, don't despair, just lift the book with both hands and bring it up rapidly into your face a few times and then keep reading... it's that important.)

By this time we'd been strolling around the courtyard while talking, and we ended up sitting on a bench near a fountain, one of those big round stones with water flowing over it.

Yvonne began by giving me an example from football. (She had figured out how to talk to people in language they found meaningful.) "You follow football so you know who Larry Fitzgerald is?"

"Of course —he's a contender for best receiver in football."

"When Fitzgerald started in the NFL, he was a very fast receiver, but that was all, and there's more to being a great receiver than speed. His coach at the time called him a 'one-trick pony.' Apparently that broke through his ego from being a college star, and Fitzgerald took it as a challenge and jokes about it. That's a tidy little criticism as a compliment story, but I mention it only as contrast to another football coach story."

We got interrupted here. One of my employees had tracked me down, apparently having heard I was in the courtyard, and came to me, telling me he had "a small crisis." I decided it was time to try out one of my new techniques, and after letting him tell me the situation, said, "That's an interesting dilemma. I have faith in you, and I'm going to be interested in how you handle it. Why don't you come up with three solutions, and if you can't decide which one to choose, come to me and we can talk them through together."

That wasn't in the category of "smelling the fish," but if I'd pulled an actual fish from the fountain and hit him with it he wouldn't have looked more stunned. He tried to object, and I might have slipped, but I caught Yvonne's eye and just seeing her watching was like that great crack from Margaret Thatcher to the first President Bush, "Don't go wobbly on me, George."

So I smiled big, repeated my instructions, and said, "This is going to be good." And I meant it. After all, they always know.

He left annoyed, and Yvonne congratulated me and pointed out that employees hate any change at first, but after he tried it, would prefer solving his own problems. "You just did him a favor."

She returned to her second football example. "This one is about Ron Marinelli, who was the Defensive Coordinator for the Bears and now for the Cowboys. He wanted to get more effort from his team. He could have run around shouting 'Hustle!' or putting cutesy mottoes on lockers, but instead he came up with a metric for hustle. He defined five things that he considered a 'loaf,' as in 'loafing.' They were things like when a defensive player gets knocked down by a blocker and stays down instead of popping up and trying to get back in on the tackle. Like I say, there were five of them. And Marinelli would watch the game tape and keep track and then post how many 'loafs' each player had.

"So, on the one hand we have the 'one-trick pony' conversation, and then with the 'loafs' we have a metric. The latter is a way to create conversations, then eventually eliminate conversations. When you create a metric, you define what you care about and want employees to care about, and there it is, a feedback mechanism. Without the metric, a football player can argue about whether or not he is trying hard or hustling. He can think the coach is being unfair or singling him out or whatever. But once you create the metric, there it is, making the vague notion of attitude into something specific.

"I talked recently with Mark Wheeler, an executive with one of the big pharmaceutical companies, who works with salespeople all over the world. He told me 'I could write a book on all the excuses of why-my-country-is-different.' But he took all the metrics the company was collecting and put them into a straightforward report for each salesperson that said, 'Here are the key indicators, here are your goals, and here's how you are doing.' Then, he could say this:

"There's no emotional debate with the boss about whether you are a good guy or a bad guy—it's there in the numbers.'

She continued with this...

———————

"Here's what I want you to understand: Let the numbers be hard and you can be gentle. Good cop/bad cop. You don't have to nag—the metric is the nag. You are the teacher, helping the person get better. You and your metrics, taken together, become a lovable hard-ass."

———————

"I do, but I'm going to have trouble applying it to my position, running training programs."

She smiled, and I knew she'd heard that one a hundred times and proven it wrong every time. "That's what you would have said about 'hustle,' right? You can't define hustle. It's an attitude. Fine, but if you can say, 'I'll know it when I see it,' then you can envision outcomes, which is a way of seeing it, and work to put a metric to it. Let's try it right now."

## Instant Metrics

She then asked me to name some possible goals for my department and me. You'll remember that I run Training for a mid-sized corporation, so my team doesn't have the measurement options companies would have, like revenues or product ratings. At the time, I was judged by an old-fashioned job review—what my boss thought of me, which boiled down to whether or not I was a pain in his butt and what compliments or complaints he heard from his fellow execs.

Yvonne pushed me, and eventually I said, "Okay, I'd like to be considered one of the top Training departments in the country."

"How will you know if you succeed?"

"If we get written up in the trade journals and invited to speak at national conferences."

"How do they pick?"

I wasn't sure. Here I was, wanting to get to those places, and I didn't even know the criteria they used. Hmmm. I had some work to do.

"Let me guess how they pick," Yvonne offered. "Someone with a good story. That takes me back to the *National Geographic* photographer and his cannibalistic butterflies. Or they choose a good a success story. And what makes a good success story? Success you can prove, which means you can measure. If you could say, for instance, 'We figured out how to double the number of people we train, without adding staff,' that's a story. Or, 'We have everyone who goes through training take a survey, and we increased our customer satisfaction scores by 50% in less than a year.' That's a story.

"Then, once you have quantifiable goals, you can start to measure your progress. You ask every person on your team to try an experiment every quarter, hoping to find some cool new methods. Soon you'll have stories. The same ones that elevate you in your profession will be told internally. The top people are held to the P&L and other numerical goals, so they'll respect your use of metrics."

That was when Yvonne told me another of the stories that will stay with me a long time.

> It was the story of a guy running hospitals and clinics in the Chicago area, Dr. Joseph Golbus. He wanted to improve the business by increasing the satisfaction of patients. He chose to start by focusing on a single measure, the Loyalty Score, the one that comes from asking, "Would you refer friends and family to this clinic?"
>
> He kept it simple, just one number, what researchers call "top box," meaning the percentage of people who choose the highest possible rating, in this case Strongly Agree (a five out of five).

Yvonne said of that new metric, "It doesn't sound like a big deal and wouldn't have been if it stopped there. But Golbus started putting out a report, giving each doctor his or her Loyalty Score, with the scores *for all the other doctors.*

Picture this. Just one word, Loyalty, and one number per doc, the 'top box.' But seeing a list of those results meant that the physicians, who had considered themselves above mere marketing, suddenly had pride and/or natural competitiveness kick in.

Yvonne also pointed out that once you have one number that really matters, then other numbers become more relevant. In this case, once people start to care about the "would you refer friends" measure, then they have to care about what's related to it, what drives it. Turns out, in the case of the doctors, "looks me in the eye" and "knows my name" are the best predictors of the referral rating. Knowing that, you can train doctors on those simple skills, and you can hire for them as well.

Eventually, Golbus convinced doctors that being nice wasn't just nice; it was lucrative. He showed that during a two-year span, "loyalty" rose by 20% while doctors' income rose an average of 15%. Soon their clinics were offering same-day and walk-in appointments, increased hours in the evenings and on Saturdays, and they even have a pediatric walk-in clinic open on Sunday mornings. Golbus was able to boast, "Our customers became our marketing, our sales force."

One number, and you have the start of a metrics program.

## Lean vs. Muscular

If you work in manufacturing, no doubt you've been using

Lean, or at least hearing plenty about it. At the time I met Yvonne, Lean had *not* reached my little office, and so as we walked back there, Yvonne explained to me the basics.

(Okay, this gets a tad technical. Hang in. Why? Apply what you learn in the next few pages, and you will double your salary.)

Lean grew out of the Toyota Production System, popularized by Taiichi Ohno (who helped develop it and who wrote a book on the subject). The basic idea is to take a process and turn it into a timeline. Then you figure out ways to improve the timeline, which mostly involves cutting time or cost, and that's why the most famous piece of the process is looking for The Seven Wastes. These are, quoting Ohno's book, "Waste of overproduction, time on hand (waiting), transportation, processing itself, stock on hand (inventory), movement, and making defective products." There are two ways of finding these wastes.

One is to do what's called "the five whys," which is just asking "why" five times.

Yvonne pointed out that we'd already had a great example, and to not waste time (wink), I'll remind you of the insurance agency and the 3,000 calls. Instead of adding another receptionist, Terry Richter, in effect, asked "Why so many calls?" and then "Why?" again and again, analyzing each major source of calls and why they were or were not necessary.

Second, there is simply standing and watching. As Ohno put it, "Stand on the production floor all day and watch—you will eventually discover what has to be done. I cannot emphasize this too much." And neither could Yvonne. For instance, she had analyzed a homebuilder and discovered that they spent a lot of time explaining to customers why they couldn't make changes to their new home. They turned the issue into a video for homebuyers, heading off the conversations and the disappointments.

Yvonne concluded her discussion of Ohno by pointing out, "Once a plant had improved, it was common for the managers to get a bit cocky, thinking they were doing well. Ohno says that if you think something like, 'As a whole, things seem to be proceeding reasonably,' *you are already failing to improve.* He says, 'If we allow ourselves to feel this way, we cut off any hope for progress or improvement.'" Now there's the relentlessness of a true leader.

"If You're Not Keeping Score, You're Just Practicing"

"Okay," Yvonne added, "we talked about manufacturing. Let's talk about how Lean can be used anywhere. You can create timelines for your department's reports, or classes, or accreditation. Here's how Lean looked when the state government of Georgia put it to use...

"It started with the Governor, Sonny Perdue, who was in office from 2003 to 2011. He'd been an entrepreneur and before that, a football player at the U of Georgia. So goals and numbers were part of his psyche, and so he set a big, lovably hard goal: to make Georgia the best-run state in the nation. How to get there? One way was to have the best customer service of any state. Big goal, and to that he added a bias for metrics, announcing, 'If you're not keeping score, you're just practicing.'

"Another former entrepreneur, Joe Doyle, was given the task of fulfilling his governor's customer service goal. He started keeping score: The average wait for a driver's license was two hours, the wait for action on a child support issue was fourteen weeks…on and on, one horrible number after another.

"In other words, he had big challenges and no new money to offer to state agencies. His only resource was a governor who demanded that state agencies start keeping score.

"Doyle asked each agency to name a Customer Service Champion. Naturally, he and his champions faced cynicism. He told me this…

---

'In any organization you'll find twenty percent of the employees are passionate about what they do and twenty percent are on the other end, the whiners. The battle is for the 60 percent in between—who will they listen to?'

~ JOE DOYLE

---

"Among his first efforts was an anti-whine campaign, telling each group that the motto 'Better results with existing resources' was not code for lay-offs. Instead, he announced that 'no one has ever lost a job because of this work' and that 'no one is going to be asked to work more.'

So here were Doyle and his champions, promising to improve results using this formula: same budget, same people, same hours, better results. Hmmm.

"Just as with Lean, the key step was the timeline. The employees in each of the state agencies began by mapping out every step in the process of delivering a single service. Take, for instance, a woman who came in to ask for help in getting financial support from her child's father. She'd fill out paperwork, which would, in about ten days, be put into the system, and then, after about twenty more days, result in her meeting with a caseworker, who'd assign an investigator to locate the father. Map out the timeline and you get a turnaround of fourteen weeks. However, with the map in hand, you could see that during those fourteen weeks, actual employee time spent on the typical case was about three hours.

"The employees then reconfigured the process with efficiency in mind. For instance, in the child support example, protocol dictated that the agency would assign an investigator to locate the father; however, in virtually every case, the mother knew where the father was—for some reason, it had been considered politically incorrect to just ask her. They started asking and doing everything else they could to reduce The Seven Wastes.

"The upshot is that a process that took fourteen weeks is now same-day service. And those improvements are happening in every agency in Georgia—the wait for a driver's license went from two hours to eight minutes, Medicaid applications went from nine weeks to fourteen days, the certifying of healthcare providers from eighteen months to three. I can't remember them all, but the point is that process after process could be redesigned and improved, and by the workers themselves."

Yvonne and I then had a conversation about what we could learn from Georgia. For one, Doyle and the champions didn't criticize the employees or the management, just the problem. They didn't go in to "fix" the people, just improve the processes. Indeed, given the opportunity, the employees, fixed each process. And once one process was improved, all Doyle had to do was ask, "Is there anything else you'd like to speed up or do better?" and soon his champions really were just that; they had a string of victories. Same people, better results.

———————

"If you're not keeping score, you're just practicing."

~ SONNY PERDUE

———————

## Beyond Lean

Yvonne continued, "So, we can love Lean. And why not? It's one thing you can get any management to agree to—cutting waste, getting faster and cheaper. But what worries me is that Lean's fundamental orientation is cutting. Think about the word Lean—it implies lack of fat. You cut waste; you cut fat. You get a low percentage of corporate body fat. But if you aren't careful, you get skinny instead of muscular. That's why I don't just want you to think about cutting waste, but analyzing the timeline for places to exercise creativity.

"When you do your timeline, I want you to look for the Seven Wastes and ask the five whys, but don't just cut. Look for chances to do something marvelous. In addition to wastes, come up with innovations. About each step in the timeline ask how you could cut waste, and then ask how you could make it special.

"For instance, when we looked at that homebuying timeline for a homebuilder—the one I was telling you about earlier, when we talked about 'standing and watching,' we looked at where employee or customer time was wasted. One was having a conversation about making changes in the house. This was frustrating for everyone, and nothing good came of it. But the homebuilder didn't just make the video that explained what changes could and couldn't be made; the builder went further and made custom changes a profit center. They started selling new options, and what had been a nuisance became not just a way to cut costs, but a way to increase revenues.

"Another example: When they looked at the homebuying process, the salespeople knew that customers cared about the new neighbors, and it became a common conversation. They didn't want to cut out the conversation—it wasn't a waste—but it was an opportunity to do something better. They ended up creating a Book of Neighbors, inviting buyers to include pictures and key facts, like ages of children and places of employment. Once they had the book and photos, not only could the salespeople show it to potential buyers (saving some time, perhaps) but it also allowed prospects to feel at home—with people from the same company or profession, same church, or kids of the same ages.

Yvonne concluded, "It's not just the 'five why's' looking to cut waste, but five 'what else?s' to look for ways to make it great. Think of it as not just The Seven Wastes but The Seven Inspirations. That's how you get from lean to muscular."

## The Seven Inspirations

Okay, friends, here's your reward for hanging in with me on the Lean discussion—the process I'm about to describe is something you can have real fun doing while becoming known as a creative genius.

I asked Yvonne for more detail on what she called "The Seven Inspirations." Turns out there wasn't a list of seven, just her idea of taking the time to look for ideas. When she saw that I was disappointed that there wasn't a list, she brightened and said, "Let's do the seven right now. All we need are seven things that can make an item in a timeline come alive."

So we started trying out idea-generating words and after coming up with dozens, we narrowed it to this:

# Lean Versus Muscular

# THE SEVEN INSPIRATIONS

After eliminating "the seven wastes," ask, <u>can</u> we make this...

1. **Beautiful?**
2. **Fun?**
3. **Helpful?**
4. **Educational?**
5. **Entertaining?**
6. **Valuable (revenue-generating)?**
7. **Remarkable (promoting word-of-mouth)?**

We might have included "easy," "simple," "less expensive," or "fast," but we figured that the Lean process would have already taken care of those. Our seven are about making it great, not just efficient.

Think for a minute about the builder who evaluated the homebuying process, the one who came up with the Book of Neighbors. Lean couldn't get you there, but The Seven Inspirations could have produced that idea under consideration of any one of four of the seven.

Once you try working the Seven Inspirations a couple of times, it gets easy and fun and will become a favorite part of your work.

# CHAPTER SIX:
## Respect

We were back in my office, and it was getting late in the afternoon. Yvonne looked at her watch and let out a tiny gasp. "We're going to have to pick up the pace, but that shouldn't be a problem—once you understand the mindset of being lovably demanding, these last principles should fall into place. Let's take on this next group..."

8. **Understand who's ready for a not-ready assignment.**

9. **Fear is your friend (and "Are you crazy?" is that friend winking at you).**

10. **Choose "respected" over "liked." The love comes later.**

"What do you think of my using the word 'fear'?" she asked.

"It's scary. And negative."

She pulled a face, weighing the word in her mind. "I knew I would be open to criticism for embracing the word. But when I see great management there's a little phrase that comes to mind: 'scary-good.' And with it comes clean, bright fear. This isn't worry, but exhilaration, taking a leap into uncertainty. It happens when you involve the word 'up,' as in *step up,* or *live up to.*"

She reminded me that we'd come up against the word fear when talking about the ad man David Ogilvy and how she'd asked his former employee if they feared him. While he was shocked by that question and explained how charming Ogilvy was and how loved, he admitted that they didn't fear *him*, they feared letting him down, feared failing to live up to his standards and the agency's reputation.

Yvonne said, "You don't build a reputation for exceptional work by being easygoing; you build it by setting standards that make people nervous. (Every daring endeavor makes someone nervous.) The trick is how to be demanding *and* charming. Do that, and you tap into the talent spiral—the best want to work with the best."

While that sounded super and all, I have to admit that I was getting a bit nervous, thinking about all I had to do and change, and the one piece that was the itchiest was this idea that you offset the fear that came from being demanding by being *charming*. "I'm pretty good at being likable," I told her, "but suddenly, talking with you, being likable is not an important skill. Okay. I understand your point about that. But I'm not a charmer. I can't tell a joke that puts everyone at ease or throw my arm around a shoulder and sweet-talk someone. So I'm not sure about making the leap from likable to lovable, especially while I'm handing out criticisms and asking people to raise their standards."

Yvonne leaned back, and I sensed I had disappointed her. "Not a problem. Remember, 'They always know.' People want to know why you're suddenly asking more of them. If they sense that you're doing it for personal ambition, they'll play along but never get committed. But when they sense that you're doing it for team ambition, that you believe in being special by doing something special for your customers, then the best ones will buy in and rise up. I sense that you really care, and that's why I'm still here. I respect that. Your employees will too. That's where we start, and the love comes later. The worst thing you could do is go around trying to be lovable." She gave a little shudder, and I knew what she meant.

Smiling, I said, "So I start by being scary," just joking, but she nodded.

"Scary-good. You start talking about what the team might accomplish and what each employee could contribute."

"I could use some examples."

Yvonne had plenty. For instance, Tracey Rice, an executive with Coca-Cola, whose boss had decided that the company needed to work at cutting costs and came to her and said...

---

"I need you to find me

a billion dollars."

---

"Imagine hearing that," Yvonne said. "Is that scary-good or what? You think, all at the same time, 'Are you crazy?' and 'This guy really believes in me!' and 'Is that even possible?' and 'They picked ME for this?' You get an energy rush like someone just handed you a parachute and opened the door of the plane."

(Just so you know, I learned from Yvonne that Tracey succeeded in her billion-dollar Easter egg hunt. She traveled to production facilities around the world, enlisting help and getting commitments from each unit as to the amount of savings they could contribute. She set up monthly conference call meeting for a year in advance, the Coca-Cola production world on the phone, sharing ideas. Here's a little genius idea she came up with. Tracey wanted the first calls to be big successes, to have everyone feel that the calls were going to be seriously important and useful. So she found people with production problems and people who'd solved that problem and played secret matchmaker. She set up people in one country to own up to problems while setting up others to bring the solutions. Hence, early success— they were "set up to succeed." There's that word *up* again.)

"Notice," Yvonne concluded, "the genius in asking for a billion dollars. It's scary. Sure, the company is so huge that it's not a giant percentage number, but that's why you don't use the boring percentage number."

Find me a billion dollars. Slap. Great story with some useful details, but not so relevant to a mid-manager like me. The next two, however, were closer to my corporate home...

First, a quick one.

John Compton was working for the Fort Dearborn Company, an international packaging firm. He was VP of Org Development, and one day the president, Rich Adler, stopped him in the hall and announced that he'd been thinking of expanding their training, saying, "I think we should have a Fort Dearborn University," meaning an internal facility akin to those in much larger organizations. When Compton got over being startled and agreed, the President said, "Good. Let's have it going in six months."

Yvonne told me that even as John recalled the story, his eyes sparkled. She asked if they'd made the goal, and he laughed, saying that they didn't, but they did create a first-rate facility and did so sooner than anyone thought possible. "John told me, 'I'll never forget that meeting in the hall. It was a shock, but it was exciting and energizing. I love that Rich threw out the goal. And we created something special.'"

"The reason I like that story," Yvonne explained, "was that they *didn't* meet the crazy goal, and yet it was one of the high points of John's career. It was magic because it was a scary-good project."

She then told me another story that I've found useful, her "greatness thrust upon them" story, which best explained what she means when she talks about "ready for a not-ready assignment."

David Sears was head of shipping and logistics for a magazine and software publishing company. He wasn't sure how he was doing in his work because he had recently gone from reporting to the CEO to reporting to a VP, which he hoped wasn't a kind of demotion. In fact, when the VP, Diane Carhart, invited him to breakfast, he was worried and even suspicious.

It turned out that she wanted to talk about the upcoming corporate move (consolidating four offices while moving the headquarters to a nearby city). Then, in Sears's words, "She shocked me. I dropped the pancake I was about to bite into. She said, 'I want you to be in charge of the move.'"

When he expressed his doubts, arguing that he wasn't the right person for the job, she replied, "You're smart, you have the skills, you're the only one in the company to do it."

Nice. Still, lurking in his mind was a doubt that you might share: Is this just because she didn't want to do it herself? Could he end up just being her lackey on the project?

However, she told him, and later made good on it, "You'll make the decisions. Just tell me what you decided."

Yvonne made this comment on the conversation: "Notice the past tense—it wasn't 'tell me what you decide,' meaning, 'check with me, and I'll tell you if I'm going to let you decide that.' No, it was the genuine trust of 'decided.'"

How did it work out? First, because he'd come to admire Carhart's leadership; her faith in him caused him to think, "Maybe there's something more in me than I thought." He ended up describing it as a pivotal moment in his career.

Yvonne's commentary: "You might be tempted to

think that this is not a big deal, because the company wasn't that large, and after all, it was just an office consolidation. However, it changed how David Sears saw himself and changed forever how he saw the role of a manager. He has since taken pride in offering big opportunities to his employees in the companies he has run, including hiring a friend stuck in a job loading asphalt trucks who ended up as his VP of Finance, a process Sears calls 'having greatness thrust upon him.'"

How did things turn out over the years? Sears is now CEO of YouFloral.com, a company that rated a feature on "The Today Show" for its personalized vases. Meanwhile, his old boss, Diane Carhart, went on to become COO of the food company Stonyfield Farm.

"This is a case," Yvonne observed, "where you can see a manager truly being a leader. Carhart saw the future before anyone else. She took a chance on Sears, even though he wasn't sure he was ready. And this was a highly visible assignment, having the top people at the company affected by what he was doing and looking to him to come through.

"It makes me think of that great line from tennis player Billie Jean King, 'Pressure is a privilege.' You get pressure when it's a break, or when you're stepping up to a new level, or have high expectations. That's the good fear, the clean bright fear, and figuring out who's ready for a not-ready assignment is a great way to get there."

Yvonne gave me several more examples, and this is the one that has stuck with me:

"I talked with a young woman named Trish McCune, who was working the counter at a UPS store, and a customer named Soni Dimond, who's a speaker and media-relations consultant, saw her potential and hired her. Trish was thrilled, but terrified. She'd gone from being a clerk to dealing with Dimond's clients, mostly high-ranking executives. As she put it, 'I was afraid to even answer the phone—these were college graduates calling.' Her new boss, Soni, dismissed her concerns and even began introducing Trish to executive clients by telling them, 'You need to know her.' With that little statement, she made Trish into an equal. What a beautiful gesture and one that was so simple, like switching on a new self-image."

What I love about that story is how easy it was to alter that young woman's self-image. It was a compliment that became an aspiration. Just as the right criticism can alter a career, so can the right compliment be a double kindness—an observation of good work, wrapped in a goal, often a not-ready one.

Even though I understood these principles, Yvonne told me that most people found them tough to implement—mostly just forgetting, as it's hard to remember to be scary-good. Yvonne offered me this simple formula to use as reassurance that pressuring someone really is a privilege...

---

If one definition of leadership is to cause people to grow;

And, if people grow through adversity;

Then, leadership equals adversity.

---

———————

"Think about video games. The best ones are hard, right? It takes work and skill and practice. And if you conquer the monsters, what's your reward?"

"You get to a higher level."

"Exactly. The reward is that it gets harder. The monsters get bigger and faster and scarier. That's the reward. Think about it."

———————

## The Love Comes Later

"Let me tell you a little secret," Yvonne began. "As you've seen, I have stories from sports. I have them because I know that's a great way to communicate with guys. I don't watch sports. My brother, Max Elmore, writes down sports examples and gives them to me."

She confessed that she was going to give me a great quote from a guy she wasn't sure who he was, just that he had something to do with basketball. Well, it turned out to be Jeff Van Gundy, who, when working as an NBA commentator, said this: "When your best player is the most liked player, you've got the wrong best player."

"I'm not sure," she said, "how that works in basketball, but I know that in management the goal is not being best liked, but most respected. Best liked might get the fun projects, like hosting the awards banquet, but most respected gets the important jobs, like being on the team devising corporate strategy."

She then brightened, saying, "One of the people I've met who really gets this is Gary Bridge, who was one of the top execs at Cisco. I mentioned the concept of being lovably demanding, and he immediately remarked, 'If you set out to be lovable, then the results are going to be sub-optimal.'"

Sub-optimal. Don't you love these tech guys.

He also told her, "When the group produces results, then it's easy to love the people on the team. What you read is that if you can learn to be loved, everything will be fine, but I think it's the other way—results, then love. I think the right attitude is, 'You don't have to like me; you just have to believe me.'"

Yvonne went on to tell some stories about Gary Bridge, and the most startling was this: Bridge called a guy who was on vacation with his wife and kids and told him they had a project in trouble and that he was the only one who could solve it, and Bridge wanted him to catch a plane and fly to the Middle East. The guy ended up being there four days. I don't know about you, but that didn't strike me as the path to being loved. Okay, Bridge was classy about it—he gave the guy a lot of praise and sent something to the family, but still, it was a lot to ask. However, the project was saved and the guy wrote Gary a note thanking him, calling it "one of the best experiences of my career."

Did you follow that? Bridge pulls a guy off vacation, and the guy ends up writing him a thank-you note. Slap.

She next quoted Bridge as saying, "To achieve great things, you have to be a bit extreme." One example: He argued that if you want to get people to rise up to a new level, one secret is to under-staff the project. That way, he believes, "you *cannot* do it the traditional way, and you have to throw out the nice-to-do."

I got his points, but I was going to need to work on getting to that level.

## Golden Seeds

What was easier to like was a notion Yvonne called "golden seeds," one that she said originated with Freud, and referred to some remark from a respected figure that gave a rising man or woman a new sense of self. She explained, "Rarely, however, do 'golden seeds' come in the form of an immediate career advice. Rather, they tend to change an individual's world by changing that person's self-regard, often in ways that take years to surface. Take Jim Evans, who was CEO of both BestWestern Hotels and Jenny Craig."

(He had sent her this story, so these are his own words ...)

"Early on in my career, I worked at the Ambassador Hotel in Chicago. It was run by Mr. Asterita, a legend in the business. One day he phoned me and told me to meet him in front of the hotel. I went out front and there he was, sitting in the hotel limo. He waved me in, then told the driver to take us for a drive. He spent the trip asking me about myself—first about my work, then about my life. He even asked me if I was dating anyone. I told him about a Greek girl I'd been seeing, and then he wanted to know where I took her on dates.

"This made no sense. I couldn't imagine why he wanted to know. But I answered, telling him, 'Restaurants and clubs, maybe a movie.'

"He said, 'Oh, so you're one of them,' acting disappointed.

"Confused, I asked what he meant.

"'You do the usual things at the usual places.' Then he said, 'I think you're special. And special people should go to special places. Next time try something different, like going to a lecture at the public library. Do something special."

Yvonne illuminated that story by saying, "Forget the dating advice and just imagine how either of the little sentences, 'I think you're special,' or 'Special people should go to special places' would get inside the head of a rookie executive. How could you not want to live up to that? And Jim Evans has spent his career 'living up,' in part because that 'golden seed' has served to remind him, time and again, how being an imitator is not good enough. He loves to tell the story, and every time he does it reminds him not to give in to the lure of the ordinary, but rather, seek out the exceptional in himself and in those who work for him."

"Hold on," she suddenly said. "I almost forgot why I wanted you to hear Jim's story. It wasn't just the golden seed, which is important, but that when Jim had that first meeting, he was put off by it. Here was this older guy offering him dating advice. He was even a bit resentful, and while he admired the man, he didn't particularly like him. Not then. Only much later did he realize the gift he'd been given that day. And that was the point: the love comes later."

Next, Yvonne wanted to tell me about another executive who had been schooled by an early boss in how to be demanding but lovable. "He described a time, early in his career, when he attended Friday meetings with one of the firm's leaders, and each time he left the meeting he found himself 'wanting to work the weekend.' So he decided to study that boss to figure out how he accomplished it.

"What is was, he decided, was an implicit offer: 'I'm going to make you better. Then I'll make sure everyone will notice.' And 'I'll give you one of the best projects, letting you work on the highest priority stuff. And if you take the mission, I'll trust you, and you'll trust me.' He said of that deal, 'He let you know he was giving you a break, and no way were you going to let him down.'"

If you're like me, you're thinking, Good plan, right, but not exactly *hard*. That's when Yvonne passed along what this guy had done with his mentor's wisdom, going to work for one of the big consulting firms and telling Yvonne, "I'd take a comfortable, nine-to-five guy and give him a major assignment and say, 'You can have this tomorrow, right?' He'd end up working all night."

"Did he feel bad about calling for an all-nighter?" Yvonne asked, then answered with, "Not a bit. Instead, he said, 'They had forgotten what they were capable of. We'd shake them from their sleep.' And he added, talking of later projects in his career, 'I'd set such ambitious goals that people would say, "You're kidding me, right? That's when I knew I had the right goal."

She reached over and tapped the list...

## 11. If you're certain, you've wimped out.

She then said simply, "That's all you need to know about goal-setting." Slap.

## Big Leadership

Having been sitting for hours, Yvonne stood and stretched, then began pacing as she rolled into a topic she called Big Leadership, which was a term meant to differentiate the discussion from one-on-one leadership. For this she turned to the case of Kim McWaters who heads UTI (that's Universal Technical Institute, a for-profit education company training auto mechanics and other technicians).

> McWaters started at the company right out of high school. After eighteen years, she was made CEO and announced this startling revelation: UTI was pursuing the wrong customer.

Back in fiscal 2001, UTI had six campuses and 5,900 students. They also had losses of $2 million on revenues of $92 million. That's when McWaters took over the CEO job and started insisting that, despite losing money, "Not often do people have the chance to help shape a company, an entire workforce, and an entire industry. We have the unique ability and responsibility to change people's lives for the better."

Yvonne said, "Picture it: A young woman who started out answering phones, telling the employees of a company losing millions that they were going to change an industry by changing lives. That's Big Leadership."

They did it by no longer thinking of the students as the customers—the people paying to be there—and instead focusing the organization on the companies that she wished would hire UTI graduates, companies like BMW and Mercedes. McWaters said they went from "filling seats" to "filling jobs." That meant she had to build the organization for "the needs of industry, not the wants of students." (The industry folks, for instance, said they wanted dress codes and drug testing and other things that are definitely NOT on the "wants" list of young students.)

Here's the denouement of her story: In a decade, UTI went from six campuses to eleven, from 5,900 students to 18,000, and from losing 2 million to making 22 million. Over most of that decade they've placed more than 90 percent of their graduates and even in the two years of the auto meltdown, it was over 80 percent, leading graduates into solid jobs with Porsche and Harley-Davidson, Honda and Freightliner, even NASCAR.

"Isn't that marvelous?" Yvonne asked.

"It is. I don't know how she pulled it off. I can picture all the resistance she must have gotten from both sides, the students and the administration."

"One of her mottos is 'Progress, not perfection.' When I last spoke with Kim, she mentioned that, even now, after all their success, one of her executive still hates that line, and every time she uses it, he shakes his head and says, 'That kills me.' But she had the Big Leadership and kept saying 'Progress, not perfection,' and all the while she insisted that everyone pay attention to the metrics—there are six numbers discussed in every Monday staff meeting. That's how you create a great turnaround and an organization that does, indeed, change lives.

"I'm sure she heard 'Are you crazy?' many times—or maybe it was just whispered behind her back—but you know she was second-guessed. And I suspect people who didn't believe in her Big Leadership found other places to work. She's very likable, but she had to tell people things they didn't like hearing. That didn't matter to her; she showed everyone the Big Goal and the metrics to get there. They didn't love her plan, but had to respect where she wanted them to go; the love came later."

# CHAPTER SEVEN:
## One Sentence

We were down to just one last item on Yvonne's list of laws, and while we'd been together for most of the day, I hated for her to go. So when she tapped Number 12—

### 12. One sentence is worth a thousand meetings.

—and said, "I suspect this one should be obvious by now," I did a windshield-wiper with my head to suggest doubts.

"The full statement would be, 'One picture is worth a thousand words, but one sentence is worth a thousand meetings.' I came up with that line after watching some great leaders in action. They use language differently than mere managers. They take ideas and encapsulate them into a memorable phrase or sentence and then repeat it. Like 'Progress, not perfection.' And remember all the great lines from Jenny Lang, the auto exec? Recall that I even slipped into the list one sentence of her mom's that could make a huge difference in a lot of personal lives as well—the one about 'There are going to be times you hate your husband—it will pass.' That's true for your work and coworkers too. You could have ten meetings about what a jerk your Sales Manager is, or remember that sentence with the word 'management' inserted for husband.

"Now, there are some sentences that become a fulcrum which lifts the organization's culture. Sometimes it's Big Leadership, like a sentence from Keith Van Scotter, who runs Lincoln Paper and who keeps telling everyone in the company, 'We need to improve faster than the competition.' He calls it 'a mantra that everyone in the company can recite.' Simple, yes, but they all know what it means—that they need to get beyond world-class followership and into real industry leadership.

"Same with the folks at California Edison. They have a little sentence that seems hardly worth repeating—'Lead the way.' Seems like execu-babble, just happy talk, till you meet someone working there and hear that phrase used reverently. It guides the culture. It reminds everyone to innovate, to be first." Here Yvonne interrupted herself to point out that a little sentence can serve to do the dirty work of the hard-ass. Instead of saying to someone, "That doesn't seem creative," you can say, "I'm glad you're working on this, now we have to figure out how to get it to the point where it leads the way." The sentence becomes the standard, and it ends conversations and eliminates meetings.

At the other end of the spectrum, there are sentences that pop up for a single project, which Yvonne illustrated with this example...

"Scott Wells was running a thriving horse-racing track in Oklahoma when he heard that the Disney movie *Secretariat* was going to be released. He called his marketing team together and told them that this was a big opportunity to do something special to market the track. He instructed them to come up with a plan and gave them a two-word goal: 'Impress me!'

"That instruction became a standing joke, but it also became a very serious challenge. They had so many ideas that Scott finally told them, 'I said, Impress me, not Break me.' But they pulled it off nicely. They got the horse that played Secretariat in the movie and the jockey who played Ron Turcotte, and they got Turcotte himself, the man who rode Secretariat, and did a special preview screening of the movie. They set all sorts of revenue records. And I'm confident that 'Impress me!' will enter into the vocabulary of the track, altering the culture.

Yvonne finally stopped pacing and sat, saying, "I saved for last a line that's just right for you. There's a simple sentence that can guide a department. You remember I told you about Prometric, the company that does professional qualification testing around the world?"

"That was the woman who set standards for criticism, right?"

"Holly Dance. But I also met at Prometric an inspired young man, James Lee, who told me of the time he took over Prometric's help desk—the people who get the calls whenever there's a problem with administering a test, anywhere in the world. The tests are almost all on computers, so Lee's staff was seen, in his words, as 'tech geeks solving problems.' But Lee redefined the group. After all, these are people taking tests like the CPA exam, something they've spent months or years preparing for. Every technical problem was a matter of people taking-or-not-taking an exam, one that might determine the course of their professional lives. So he started saying, 'We save the candidates.' Then, he started calling the people in the department 'guardian angels.'

"He didn't say so, but I'll bet there were people who didn't want the new label, who didn't want the pressure of working at the 'angel' level, people who didn't understand that 'pressure is a privilege.' And I bet they found new jobs. Meanwhile, speaking of new jobs, I heard that James got a major promotion, heading a larger group and got a VP title to go with it."

Yvonne sat up straighter, and I knew she was set to deliver a juicy comment...

———————

"So he gave the people who worked on the help desk a new choice: Which would you rather spend your days doing, solving tech problems or saving candidates? Being a geek or a guardian angel?

"And here's where it gets really good: When you redefine the group and its work, you take leadership and pass it around, give it to everyone on the team. The team is pre-led because the thought-process has been pre-thought.

"Picture how that transforms the leaders role: Pre-led."

———————

Yvonne had given me the 12 sentences that we'd spent the afternoon discussing, and I could see why she called them "The 12 Laws" —most of the issues that came to me as a manager could be answered by one of those bits of encapsulated wisdom. Those sentences freed up my time to work on new ideas and new goals, so I have time for the Seven Inspirations and the rest. My department isn't just led; it's pre-led. Slap.

# CONCLUSION

I was never sorrier to see someone leave my office than when Yvonne packed up her notes and stood. I told her I'd walk her out, and I walked her all the way to her red Jaguar.

As we walked, we chatted. She gave me one last example, one last gift. She told me of an old friend, Jim Fickess, a former newspaper guy now in corporate communications.

---

Jim was reminiscing about an old boss, Marji Ranes, who'd aggressively pushed her team. Not long after she'd left to take a better job in a new city, Jim and some other editors were talking about how hard they'd been working. One said, "We worked even harder when Marji was here," to which Jim replied, "When Marji was here, we wanted to."

---

When we reached her car, she told me she'd like an email from me in six weeks with a progress report. I said that I'd gladly send it. I quickly added that she had indeed given me a great gift, just as she'd promised, and I would work on finding a way to offer her something in return. She gave that little Diane Sawyer half-smile, and let her eyes twinkle, and said, "Make your team great. Impress me."

## POSTSCRIPT—My Career Adventure After Resigning From Club Mediocre

You might be curious as to what transpired after that day with Yvonne.

The best thing I did, as mentioned earlier, was put the handwritten list of "The 12 Laws" in a plastic sleeve and leave it out on my desk. It became a joke within the department that I'd refer to the list for answers, but it was no joke to me.

I started changing the department by figuring out how to make sure my department was *not* a commodity. I'd had a good start with Yvonne, with the Big Leadership goal of being one of the best training departments in the country, and that became the first of several.

I decided to present the new goals employee by employee. (Here's the bleak truth: I was afraid that if I had them in a group, they'd rebel and argue and I'd then back down and look the fool.) Even going one-by-one, I was nervous before the first meeting. My worry was wasted—what worry isn't?

I chose my best and brightest, a young woman who seemed to me to be most likely to be an ally in the pursuit of being special. I explained about smelling the fishes and how we had slipped into inadvertent mediocrity and then eased into my new big goals. I expected her to be a tad intimidated by these scary-good standards, but she jolted me by saying, "It's about time." What? (First Yvonne and now her—what is it with these New Women startling me with their frankness?)

We both laughed, both enlivened by this new candor, and before long she was pulling out her fish and confiding that she'd contemplated changing companies because she felt that our department, not being one of the notable ones in the profession, was not going to help her advance her career, and by implication, that she was stuck at her job level within the company because her boss wasn't going anywhere—that boss was, of course, ME. Slap. Needless to say, she was eager for an adventure into the new, and she instantly became my closest ally in our transformation.

Most of the other meetings with employees went well—all but two were eager to be part of something special, especially when I explained we were going to do it without putting in more hours. What really helped was when I got each of them to discuss what it would do for all our careers to be part of something special. They weren't so happy when I told them I'd put together some new metrics that would keep track of the cost per training hour, course satisfaction scores, and some other, specialized measures.

I told them that we were going to raise customer satisfaction while decreasing cost-per-hour by one-third. How? I wasn't sure, but I told them about doing timelines and then analyzing every step of the process.

Further, I informed them that each needed an individual specialty, and I would work with them to find one. This process took weeks, but I refused to let them opt out. And a good thing. For instance, one of our guys had once wanted to do animation and was connected to a program at the local college. We were able to get some wild and entertaining materials developed inexpensively, cheaper than our usual boring videos. Another of our people decided to become an expert on excellent customer service, and we soon had ongoing classes that included visiting great service providers, the coolest hotels and retail stores, and studying the behind-the-scenes operations and coaching—we were no longer just passing on the conventional wisdom, but helping our corporate colleagues learn from geniuses and apply what they learned to their jobs. I soon had a sentence of my own that I began using: Learn from all; imitate none.

When we did the timelines, we had a breakthrough—we figured out ways to go from classroom lectures to onsite learning. When we devised an ROI class, we went to the company location with the best ROI and got the manager to give a lecture/tour, which some people attended in person and some via webcast. Our effectiveness soared while costs dropped.

Once we started getting metrics back, we discovered which of our programs were weakest, and we found ways to eliminate some, replacing them with the fun, animated online videos, and ways to make others creative. The Seven Inspirations worked, and it became something employees looked forward to. We used to design a class by pulling out the outline of some previous class and figuring out the easiest way to make it work as a new class; now we ask ourselves, How can we make this new class inspired?

(Think about this: Which meeting would you rather attend? Slap.)

On a personal level, I was spending less time doing the old management chores and instead doing real leadership. Executives around the organization noticed we were doing something new. Suddenly I was invited to corporate meetings

I'd been left out of, and I was there because everyone expected me to come up with creative ideas. And I did. (It's a matter of practicing with timelines and The Seven Inspirations, of course, but it's also just taking the time to get beyond the obvious first answer. I don't tell the executives around here how easy it is—let them think it's voodoo.)

I also made a point tc send everyone invitations to my speeches and copies of the interviews and articles in the trade press. There were plenty of these—I had my training department versions of the "cannibalistic butterflies" to discuss, and it quickly switched from me offering my work to professional organizations to them asking for it. It became something of a distraction, so I've sent employees to represent the department and they love/hate the assignments. Actually, I need to get out of the habit of referring to "the department" —I've gotten two promotions, so I now run four of them.   (And my ally, the woman who said "It's about time!" to my goals, has also had two promotions—Am I pulling her or is she pushing me? Yes.)

Each time I've been given another group, I do the same process—the Big Goals, the timelines, Lean and Muscular (especially the Seven Inspirations), smelling the fish, and the refusal to be ordinary that comes from being an anti-bureaucrat. I went from liked to respected. In fact, it's funny to me that some of the new employees start out fearing me, and I've even had a couple resign in anticipation of my leadership because they've heard about the fish and "compliments" and mandatory greatness, and they don't want to work that hard. Let 'em go. I tell them that it's not about working more, just differently. But if they fear change, I don't want them.

Looking back over what I've written here to summarize what I've accomplished, there's one little phrase that I like best, that is how I think of what we do in my teams: MANDATORY GREATNESS. Slap.

# THE 12 LAWS

1.  You and your team are a commodity product until you prove otherwise.

2.  Leadership is a magnificent intolerance.

3.  Bureaucracies evolve; organizations devolve.

4.  Criticism is a compliment.

5.  Never trust a manager who loves everything you do.

6.  Stop and smell the roses, yes, but sometimes you've got to stop and smell the fish.

7.  They ALWAYS KNOW.

8.  Understand who's ready for a not-ready assignment.

9.  Fear is your friend (and "Are you crazy?" is that friend winking at you).

10. Choose "respected" over "liked." The love comes later.

11. If you're certain, you've wimped out.

12. One sentence is worth a thousand meetings

# ACKNOWLEDGEMENTS

Having read the book, you know that we have assembled and built upon the wisdom of the leaders we have encountered in our writing, speaking, and consulting. We are grateful for their openness and willingness to share their knowledge and experiences.

We are also grateful to those who gave of their time and expertise during the creation of this book: Kathy Chandler, Steve Brown, Bobette Gorden, Bob Cialdini, Sandy Dauten, Jim Fickess, Janet Traylor, Bill Dunphy, Steve Chandler, Mark Nykanen, Alicia Holder, Paula Wigboldy, Greg Barrette, and especially Jim Evans.

We also thank the people at King Features, who syndicate our newspaper column, and all the newspaper editors who bring it to readers.

# FOR MORE INFORMATION

You can reach Dale at dale@dauten.com
or J.T. at jt@careerhmo.com.

If you are interested in seminars or having Dale and J.T. present to your organization or conference, contact Paula at 480-785-2886.

# THE AUTHORS

## DALE DAUTEN

As founder of The Innovators' Lab®, an organization devoted to developing and testing new ideas in management and marketing, Dale has done idea-generation work with dozens of organizations, including Honeywell, General Dynamics, Caterpillar, and NASA. His consulting work includes educational programs for Certified Innovation Mentors, and his work on creating a culture of innovation yielded a patent-pending new advance on brainstorming called BrainTouring™.

Dale has been researching achievers since his student days at Arizona State and Stanford University's Graduate School of Business. His early work prompted a government publication to call him a "guru" to White House staffers, and since then, his books have developed a following worldwide, especially in Japan.

In addition to co-writing with J.T. O'Donnell the country's leading career newspaper column, "J.T. & Dale Talk Jobs," for many years Dale wrote the syndicated newspaper column "The Corporate Curmudgeon" and has written seven previous books. *Mandatory Greatness* most closely resembles his most popular book, *The Gifted Boss,* in its 15th printing in the U.S. and published in eleven foreign editions.

He lives in Phoenix, Arizona.

## JEANINE TANNER "J.T." O'DONNELL

J.T. is founder and President of the leading career advice site/blog, Careerealism.com and for the provocative site CareerHMO, known as "the cure for chronic career pain." She has assembled a team of career coaches who, as approved topic experts, contribute to the sites, allowing daily updates to the content.

She describes herself as being a "field expert" on careers and workplaces, working with individuals as a career strategist and corporations as a trainer.

In addition to her work on "J.T. & Dale Talk Jobs," she is frequently quoted in major newspapers, including *The Wall Street Journal, The New York Times, USA Today,* and many others.

She is a graduate of Tufts University in Human Factors Engineering, and after several years in corporate life, has headed her consulting/coaching firm since 2001.

She lives near Boston.

Made in the USA
Lexington, KY
24 October 2013